Spiritual Living in a Material World

Morton Kelsey

Spiritual Living in a Material World

A Practical Guide

New City Press
Hyde Park, New York

Dedication

To Chiara Lubich
whose life and writing
have led countless thousands
on the spiritual journey

*Many thanks to John Neary for his editorial help
and to Linda Kalkwarf for word processing the final manuscript*

Published in the United States by New City Press
202 Cardinal Rd., Hyde Park, NY 12538
©1998 Morton Kelsey

Cover design by Nick Cianfarani

Library of Congress Cataloging-in-Publication Data:
Kelsey, Morton T.
    Spiritual living in a material world : a practical guide / Morton Kelsey.
     p. cm.
    Includes bibliographical references.
    ISBN 1-56548-105-4 (pbk)
    1. Spiritual life—Christianity. 2. Christian Life—Anglican authors.
I. Title.
  BV4501.2.K269 1998
  248.8—dc21   97-52201

Printed in Canada

Contents

We cannot be sufficient unto ourselves. We are created for the connection with others, for the connection with the cosmos, for the dynamic connection among ourselves and God. When we ask for connection, we are often met by silence. But if we listen, the silence sings to us.

Jeffery Burton Russell
A History of Heaven

Introduction

Nearly two thousand years ago a prophet began to proclaim an incredible new message, which was to change all human history. Jesus of Nazareth cried out: "The kingdom, God's holy fellowship, is at hand — within us and around us. We can live in it now. In spite of what happened to John the Baptist, God will not be defeated." The communion of saints and the angelic realm, Jesus announced, are real. We can taste it and live in it now, and it will last forever.

That prophet preached and taught and healed. His message remained the same: God's love would conquer even the Roman Empire that soon crucified him. Jesus experienced the depth of human agony and died. But he did not stay dead; he appeared again and again to his terrified disciples. Finally they realized that Life and Love had conquered death. Jesus then ascended into God's fellowship and became available to all of us in all time and space.

In a recent book Reynolds Price, the poet, novelist and literary critic, presents a fresh, new translation and introduction to the Gospels of Mark and John. He declares that there are no other books in human literature like these Gospels; no one could have fabricated the events described in these books. These books alone have helped Price to trust God — even in his darkest moments.[1] Literature has again turned to God and the Bible for inspiration.

Jesus lived, died, and rose again in the fullness of time. Jesus came among us when everything was ready for God to be revealed in human history. God wanted all human beings to know the depth of divine love; God prepared a people who lived at the cross-roads of the ancient world, a people who would gradually take that message all over the earth.

Unfortunately, Jesus' followers have not always lived according to the heavenly kingdom Jesus described. How can we share that divine fellowship more fully? In other words, how can we live in the kingdom now? How can we meditate and contemplate on the meaning of God's love — not only in eternity but *now* as well? How can we relate to the loving God revealed in the risen and ascended Jesus?

Guideposts and Suggestions for the Spiritual Journey

Jesus said, "I am the way," and he invites all people to follow him on a spiritual adventure. But the wisest person our world has ever known also warned his followers that "the gate is narrow and the road is hard that leads to life, and there are few who find it" (Mt 7:14). Since the way is so difficult, we need all the guidance and help we can get if we are going to bring all parts of our lives into the splendor and joy of God and the kingdom of heaven. Certainly the goal is more than worth the difficult journey, but we need to bring all of ourselves to the task — our love, patience, forgiveness and persistence. We also need human companionship to help us on the journey. Any long pilgrimage is easier with companions on the way. The ship, so often used as a symbol of Christian fellowship, needs all hands if it is to reach the harbor, to come into the presence of God and the communion

8

of saints. When storms come, we need loving fellowship if we are to weather them.

It should already be clear that I am talking of God as a real, immediate experience; there is really no point in writing or talking about the spiritual realm unless ordinary men and women can have a direct experience of God and the eternal divine fellowship. If God can only be thought about but never experienced, then the discussion had better be left to theologians and philosophers, while we get on with the business of adjusting our lives as best we can to a shadowy existence and to the material universe in which we are caught. Prayer, from such a viewpoint, would be futile, since prayer is basically seeking fellowship with the loving God Jesus revealed, coming to know the reality of which Wesley sang: "Love Divine, all loves excelling . . . Enter every trembling heart."

I know what it means to be caught in a meaningless materialistic world in which there is no place for the love of Jesus to touch us. My father was a very fine man, but he was an engineer who did not believe that there was any spiritual realm — or at least that humans had any contact with it. My mother did not have the background to stand up to my father's materialistic faith. He believed that when we died, we left behind only dust and ashes.

When I was twenty-one years old, my mother died, leaving me in a dark abyss. I was studying philosophy in a graduate school where my professors were professed atheists who scoffed at Christian belief. Finally I realized I must find meaning and a way to experience God. I decided that the best place to seek this experience was in a seminary, so I found a seminary and enrolled in it. There I discovered one wise and profound Christian writer, Baron von Hügel, who showed the reality of religious experience in the life of Saint Catherine of Genoa. For me, studying Von Hügel's work was far deeper than studying with the agnostic professors. I also found a group of students who met quietly together to pray before our daily liturgical service. However, there were no classes on how we might open ourselves to God or to the spiritual world that God had created. And when our little prayer group scattered after we graduated from seminary, my sense of God's presence flattened. Without fellowship, it is easy to grow slack in opening ourselves to God; we need one another to support each other in the spiritual journey.

Later in my ministry I realized that I had lost touch with my spiritual roots. Our church was growing and my family was well. But my wife knew that something was wrong. I was too busy, and I was trying to minister from my own wisdom and strength rather than as an instrument of God's loving Holy Spirit. I found several writers who showed that the human soul is just as real as the human body and even more mysterious. I began to see that our souls need to keep in touch with God if we are to have health in spirit, mind, and body, as well as in our relations with other people. Fritz Künkel in *In Search of Maturity* and Dorothy Phillips in her excellent anthology *The Choice Is Always Ours* make the same point. In a more explicitly religious vein, my friend John Sanford, in his book *The Kingdom Within,* makes a similar point: He describes the incredible soul-wisdom to be found in Jesus' parables about the kingdom of God.

The most significant secular book that spoke to me about the soul and the experience of God was Carl Jung's *Modern Man in Search of a Soul*. It smashed open my materialistic prison and let me hear the unfathomably profound message of Jesus. Jung and I exchanged letters. He invited me to visit with him in Switzerland while I was there. I asked him what psychological practice was nearest to his own, and he replied, "The directors of conscience in late nineteenth-century France — people like Abbé Huvelin." Christianity has always prepared some priests and lay people to know and understand the depth of the human soul. These men and women are trained to help us find our way to deeper and deeper relationship with one another and with God and the spiritual world.

When we realize we are lost, we need this kind of help. We may encounter signposts that give us directions to keep us on the path, but sometimes these signs are nothing more than cuts made in the bark of trees to indicate a trail in a forest. We may need a living human expert to show us how to find and use these signs. Sometimes we need elaborate maps as well as simple signposts. More and more people are seeking some guidelines for the spiritual pilgrimage.[2]

It is possible to develop a sustained and creative relationship with God, the spiritual world, and one another. This is not only possible — as we shall point out in the pages that follow, finding God is imperative. Civilization — the very survival of the human race — hangs in the balance. A materialism which maintains that there is no God or spiritual world wipes out all meaning and value for each of us. It also destroys a basic teaching of Jesus: the belief in the divine value of *every* human being.

During the cultural revolution in China, a young communist soldier was burning Bibles. He wondered why this book was so dangerous and decided to keep one and read it. For the first time he could imagine that there might be a loving God who created the universe and gave infinite value to every human soul. Jesus' assurance that God loves every human being converted this Chinese Red Guard to Christianity.

We help others know the reality of the love of God as they see it flowing from us. But we have to know the loving God before we can fully become people of God's fellowship. Asking of God — petition — is one form of relationship, but in full fellowship with God we have a sense of God's presence and of a divine response to our presence and concerns as well.

In other books I have described the reality of God's kingdom and the many different ways in which God seeks to enter and direct our lives. I have also outlined various ways we can be open to God.[3] Before we start any long journey (and the spiritual one can reach into eternity), we need to be certain that we are ready and willing to take it. Before the narrow gate of which Jesus spoke, two warning signs are posted.

Warning Signs

The first warning tells us that the journey before us is difficult. Sustained living in God's fellowship requires our full commitment. It requires more than just the mind, more than our self-satisfied picture of ourselves. We will need to look at our angers and fears. We will need to be willing to be wholly transformed by our fellowship with the risen Jesus and our companions on the way. It is easy for most people to have a single-shot experience of the Divine Fellowship (it is commonplace that there are no atheists in foxholes), but it is a gigantic task to live lives in which fellowship with God and our brothers and sisters is an integral and daily part of life. However, most really vital human beings like challenges; they add zest to life. Christian life and fellowship offer the greatest challenge we can face.

It is far more difficult for us in our time and culture to find a way into continued fellowship with the loving God than it was for those to whom Christianity first spoke. The men and women of the first century (like the Chinese soldier) believed that there was a realm of spirituality that touched and influenced human lives (though it was sometimes hostile and sometimes friendly — one could not count on it). The gospel message had only to convert their image of God and show them the moral chaos in which they were living.

People living in that age were looking for a moral religion, and many came to Jewish synagogues for guidance. It is a more difficult task, however, to reach those brought up in our modern secular and materialistic culture. First of all we need to break through the modern materialistic world view that controls men and women of today and help them realize that there is indeed an amazing spiritual realm as well as the incredibly complex physical one. This is a job in itself; it is easier to change our moral attitudes and actions than to transform the basic view of modern culture upon which our lives are built. But changing our intellectual world view is only an initial step; what we actually *do* about stepping out upon the spiritual journey with a rule of life is a better indication of what we truly believe than the statements of belief that we make. Do I believe in God? What do I do about it? What is my religious practice? What we believe is better shown by what we do than by what we say.

The second warning sign pictures danger. If Jesus and the Church are right, then we will find that there are negative and destructive spiritual powers as well as benign ones. We need Jesus as our guide as well as a human partner to keep us on track. How often in the twentieth century whole nations have been engulfed with destructiveness. Whenever our spiritual practice does not contribute to our love for other human beings, we are not following Jesus on his narrow pathway.

Real Christianity is a mature and balanced religion; it stresses our spiritual life, our physical life, and our social life as one integrated whole. In some ways Christianity is the most materialistic of all major religions: It speaks of the spirit, but within the framework of the material world in which hurting, confused human beings need compassion and help to minister to themselves and to others. (This is why Christians need a fellowship of like-minded people.) The central message of Christianity is that God became a human being so that human beings might share in divinity: so they might be one.

Jesus was born, he taught and loved, and then he was crucified and rose again physically. This continues to be expressed in the central worship service of Christianity, the eucharist or communion service. In the liturgy, bread (from grain sowed and tended by the sweat of human toil) and wine (pressed from the fruit of the green vine) become carriers of God's spirit and love. This is balanced spirituality: Christianity in its truest form stresses both the material and spiritual. God created both heaven and earth, and our faith is not just a spiritual religion in which individuals lose themselves in spiritual bliss and forget the world and its people. It is not a flight of the alone to the alone.

Signposts

Strangely enough, this is one reason that many people today are dissatisfied with Christianity. Many people don't want to deal with the problem of evil and the cross, with poverty and war, with sickness and pain. Many people want all reality to be spiritual and good, the point of view of some of the great Eastern religions. How, then, do we Christians learn to avoid spiritual evil and accept God's love for us with all our faults as we grow more fully into the mysterious love of God? I offer some signposts that can lead us more and more deeply into the love of God and one another.

These suggestions have been culled from many different sources. They spring mainly from my Christian heritage: forty years of reading the Bible and devotional classics. They have been tested in the crucible of my own struggles, though I have often been faulty in observing them. I have already noted that some modern psychologists have opened my eyes to the incredible depth of myself and to the significance of the risen Jesus. Psychology, however, did not bring me salvation. That came through the risen, ascended, cosmic Christ, who died and rose again for us. Jesus' death and resurrection defeated the powers of evil and gave me a way to find victory and eternal hope.

In addition, for forty-five years I have been listening to people who have come to me seeking direction on the religious journey. The suggestions I offer have been filtered through the experience of these people and are largely the result of their sharing their stories. I have learned as much from those who have opened their souls to me as from any other source.

The suggestions I offer overlap one another. The process of spiritual growth is an organic one that can never be completely analyzed. These suggestions are not a blueprint for a sealed-in relationship with God and the spiritual world. There is no such blueprint, and we must use these suggestions with caution and see which ones are for us and help us grow. Different people find different ways to grow in God's kingdom that is among us and within us and beyond us.

These suggestions, then, are not a logical system or a set of principles to be analyzed. Their real value lies in being used; they are a plan for action. We grow in fellowship with God's spiritual kingdom *not just by thinking, but by building fellowship with others on the spiritual journey and by going into training.* These signposts are like the practical ones which athletes need to follow. They are practical suggestions for spiritual training for a long pilgrimage.[4] In an editorial in a popular news magazine, one writer speaks of the spiritual hunger that is evident in America today and our need to deal with it.

Act As if the Kingdom of Heaven Is Real

As we enter the narrow gate, we meet the first signpost on the journey toward religious fulfillment: an affirmation that the spiritual realm is real. This suggestion may seem perfectly self-evident. But often the most obvious ideas are the very ones that we miss. Before we can go very far spiritually, we need to accept at least tentatively that Jesus was correct in his proclamation. The kingdom of God, the kingdom of heaven, is indeed at hand, among us and within us. This open attitude is essential.

It is like prospecting. No one ever brought in a wildcat well or hit a bonanza mine who had no idea of the possibility that there was some oil or some gold to be had. Much the same holds true for God's kingdom. The Holy One does not force us to enter the kingdom. Paul met the risen Christ on the Damascus road and could have said his experience was nonsense; Ananias, who welcomed Paul into the Christian fellowship, could have refused to believe that God would use this violent persecutor of the Church. But both of them believed God could use anyone for the kingdom of heaven. After real training, Paul became one of the greatest missionaries of the Church. If we do not even dream that there are vast caverns beneath the surface of life, we are not likely to find an entrance to them.

We must be open to the possibility that an unfathomable and divine reality lies beneath and beyond this material world.

A man invited me to lunch, and even though I forgot his invitation, he graciously called me and we met and talked of his inner longing. In his middle seventies, this man had come to the conclusion that something was missing in his life. He had been turned off by the religion of his youth and by his knowledge of the religious wars that had devastated Europe, but he was still open. As we talked, I suggested that there are as good reasons for belief in the reality of a loving God as there are for not believing.

He began to look back over his life and see that he had never been exposed to the rich, deep reality of the loving Christ who died and rose again for us. He tentatively returned to the church of his childhood. He found that it struck chords of meaning. He began to read some of the great spiritual writers of the Church, and some modern ones who were trying to present their experiences to people of today.

As the man explored the religious path more and more, his conviction grew. This is not to say he became absolutely certain; if we wait until we come to complete certainty, we may never act, never take the first step that leads through the narrow gate. The leader of the man's church fellowship was a very wise and understanding priest, who encouraged lay people to meet together to organize and build a fellowship and then a church. The community was small, and many of the people had known each other for years but had not realized that their friends had the same religious concerns and interests as they did. Thus, the man found a group who wrestled together with the problems that confront people on the spiritual journey. As I have already pointed out, the religious journey is not a solitary venture; we need to find companions on our way. One of the main reasons for churches is to provide this fellowship.

Jesus did not preach and then disappear. He gathered a group of twelve followers whom he trained. When he had risen from death and ascended into heaven, his disciples gathered together. After selecting another apostle to take the place of Judas, each of these disciples then trained other disciples, and all set out to the far corners of the Roman Empire. This is the way real Christianity grows — not just by preaching or ideas but by fellowship, companionship in prayer, and service to others. By this kind of ministry Mother Teresa gathered together thousands who wanted to live out their Christianity among the poor and dying of India.

Again, action is more important than intellectual certitude; if we believe that we must be absolutely sure about God's kingdom before considering it and trying out its reality, then we may well wait forever and never find its reality. Conviction that God's kingdom is indeed among us (embodied by our spiritual companions) and within us is often called *faith*. This gift is given because we have set our hearts and put our energy into finding the reality of God's kingdom of love.

This takes action. We can learn much from the scientists of our time, who operate in a pragmatic rather than purely intellectual way. They realize that they don't understand our physical, material world, and they try one path and then another until they discover an answer that leads to another question. As their knowledge grows, they realize how mysterious God's world truly is. Another example is that of fisherfolk. They do not know where the fish are, but they keep on fishing until they find their catch.

Jesus is very clear about how necessary it is to keep on seeking if we are to find and be found by God: "So I say to you, Ask and it will be given you; search and you will find; knock and the door will be opened for you." Jesus then points out that no parent would give destructive gifts when a child asks for good ones. He concludes with these words: "How much more will the heavenly Father give the Holy Spirit to those who ask him!" (Lk 11:9-13; Mt 7:7-11).

God wants the companionship of every one of us. But how do we ask things of God? Most of us find it very easy to pray when we are in great need; indeed, sometimes this is the only way that we can survive. We call this "petition" — we cry out, "Lord, oh God, be with me, I cannot manage my own life by myself." Sometimes we wonder why our prayers are not answered, but Jesus' deep insight is that God does indeed want to hear from us; God listens.

In his book *A Whole New Life*, Reynolds Price tells of a vision he had when he was very sick and in great pain. Jesus came toward him as he stood by the Sea of Galilee, poured water over his head, and said: "You will be healed." Months went by with no change and Price kept up his call: "How long, oh Lord, how long!" During his period of waiting, he drew hundreds of pictures of Jesus; this was a kind of prayer, an expression of his experience of Jesus' presence. Finally healing came, and Price continued his writing and shared his faith.

Sometimes the answer comes quickly and unexpectedly. A friend told me the story of his desperation. He was given a company to run that he didn't want, and the company was in real trouble. Finally he went into his office, closed the door, sat down at his desk, and muttered to himself, "There is nothing that I can do except pray. It probably won't help, but any other alternative would be destructive." So he cried out, "Lord, help!" The echoes of his own voice had hardly died away when these words came to him: "Create the conditions whereby individuals may develop to the maximum of their capacity within the opportunities at hand." He said: "What Lord?" The same words came again. These words became his guideline and signpost. A sense of community developed and the business turned around.

God can speak to us no matter who we are. Even the most self-centered prayer at least acknowledges that God is there waiting to hear from us. When we pray for others, we can lift them into God's presence and we ourselves can share in the divine light and love that shines on them. Many people find it helpful to keep a list of those they want to pray for — though letting the list get too long can be counter-productive, as the list becomes a burden.

Times of quiet, of petition and intercession, become evidence to us that we are actually on the spiritual journey. In these times we are not just thinking about God, we are reaching out in spirit and also listening. Any of us can enter upon this religious way, no matter what we think or doubt. The more we come into God's presence alone and with our spiritual companions, the less frequent our doubts become.

Some people believe that because they have doubts, they are not welcome in any Christian community. Nothing could be further from the truth. Even Jesus' disciples doubted. In any real community, doubters will be welcomed with open arms. Christians have much to share; the more they have been touched by the incredible love and mystery of the risen and ascended Jesus, the more they want to share the good news that the kingdom of God is within and around us — stretching out into eternity. It is lukewarm Christians who are given a low spiritual score, not seeking, honest doubters.

Different people have different needs. Every church worthy of its name needs to have prayer and fellowship groups as well as study and work groups.[1]

In the ancient world the Jesus movement grew rapidly and with great power, partly because peoples and cultures were linked in new and dynamic ways. Roman roads linked cities from Turkey to Great Britain, from North Africa to the Rhine River. The Jews had scattered to cities throughout the Empire, and wherever they went, they had synagogue services. Many people of that time were seeking a moral religion, and when they came to the synagogues, Jews welcomed these spiritually hungry pagans to their worship and fellowship (see Acts 10). The strict ritual laws and the Jewish practice of circumcision, however, kept most of these people from becoming Jews, and these Gentiles attracted to Judaism were called "God-fearers."

Soon many dynamic, excited, transformed Jewish apostles of Jesus traveled all over the Roman Empire and proclaimed the freedom, love, and victory that

Jesus Christ had preached and lived. On their journeys the apostles first visited the synagogues and announced that the Messiah had come. And they told the God-fearers that they did not have to follow the Jewish ritual law; they could become Gentile followers of Judaism by acknowledging Jesus as Lord. These ready-made congregations accepted Jesus and were the first Gentile Christian churches. They formed communities, and in his letters Paul gives us an honest glimpse of how he organized some of these new churches and kept in touch with them. The Acts of the Apostles gives further information by one of Paul's companions. Being a Christian without being in a community was unthinkable in the early Church; these early Christians risked their lives to meet regularly with their communities in worship.

One of the best ways, then, to show that we are trying to act as if the spiritual world is real is to find some Christian fellowship that is trying to grow in the spirituality of genuine prayer, love, and service. We need spiritual friends. Such groups can consist of two or three, or of a larger group, in a deeply loving and committed church. However, no Christian should be lonely, and a friendly greeting at the church door before or after a worship service is not enough. *We need Christian fellowship in which we come to know each other deeply and to accept each other and work with each other.* In a church I was serving, after the weekday eucharist we had a small prayer group — and fifty years later, my wife and I still count some from that group among our closest friends! As we pray together, think together, work together, get to know each other, we share in real life-changing experiences that tend to wash away our doubts.

We need great worship services, but we also need prayer-love fellowship groups. Many of the great renewal movements in the Church have occurred when small groups have met and shared their experiences of the loving Christ. After World War II, Chiara Lubich brought this vision of fellowship, service, and spirituality in her writing and in the Focolare Movement. From Italy it has spread all over the world. The Church of the Saviour, using small mission groups, has reached out to the poor and lost and forsaken in Washington, D.C. The name "Methodist" is taken from the *method* that John Wesley developed so people might meet and share with one another and be empowered by the risen Jesus.

Working together, praying together, loving one another can sometimes touch the heart of the most barren skeptic. When pagans saw the lack of fear and the incredible love these first Christians showed to one another, they cried out: "Look, how they love one another!" The blood of the martyrs was indeed the seed of the Church. This love conquered even the police state that was Rome — an empire as destructive and totalitarian as some in our own time.

When we find ourselves looking for books and people and groups who are sharing a belief in the immortality of the soul and the kingdom of heaven, we have an indication that we are acting as if God's kingdom is ultimate reality. And then we begin to experience a joy that the physical world alone does not give.

Undertake the Spiritual Quest
with Serious Purpose

The second signpost we confront tells us that we are stepping into a new and marvelous world; the spiritual journey is profound and a serious undertaking. Joy and lightheartedness are the end results of the successful spiritual encounter, but they are not necessarily the attitudes with which it should begin. God's kingdom is best approached with earnestness. Those who try to enter it lightly or out of idle curiosity often find themselves on a dead-end street. This is another reason why it is so helpful to have spiritual companions on the journey, a group that knows the pitfalls so well described in John Bunyan's *Pilgrim's Progress*.

Jesus told his followers to seek, and ask, and knock, and God would give the Holy Spirit in the same way that we give good gifts to our children when they ask for what they need. He also told the disciples to keep on praying, like the widow who brought her claim for justice into court so many times that the merciless judge finally gave in just to get rid of her. Perhaps the access which we desire to God's kingdom is best given to those who are persistent. They want the love of the risen Christ so much that they never give up.

There are many different, legitimate paths to take on the spiritual journey for all of us who find the need to establish a continuing relationship with God, the communion of saints and the hosts of heaven. One of the best reasons that people are led seriously to undertake the spiritual quest is that they have been raised in a family where an atmosphere of love and prayer, honesty and peace, were constantly present. People from such families have always believed in the message of Christianity. Their prayer life is a matter of continued openness and growth in the spirit. The most important way that children are educated in the faith is by being nurtured by adults who know Jesus' gospel of love and prayer and who are living it and growing in it day by day.

People from such backgrounds have been called the once-born. For them, coming into Christian community is not the result of a major crisis. Rather, it is the result of being reared in a family living in Christian love with their children, friends, and neighbors. Quite naturally, such people want the support and fellowship that such a fellowship can give. My wife was raised in such a family. People with this background often find centering, imageless prayer most fitting for them; they rest in the quiet and find themselves in the presence of the loving God. It is even possible for people to relieve their physical pain in this way.[1]

Another way people are led to undertake the spiritual journey is by quiet, unexpected experiences of the risen Christ or the kingdom of heaven. Popping perhaps out of some ordinary situation of daily life, the experience breaks in on some people suddenly and without preparation, and has so much meaning and power that it draws them to seek further and further. Their lives, which had been drab and stale, become unexpectedly filled with spiritual light and power and new life. Then they start the quest, with the earnest wish to have constant relationship with this God of love; their experience gives them the desire to maintain this kind of joy and peace. The way of Paul and Francis of Assisi and many of the great saints of the Church has been by this kind of experience.

For still others, there is the way of obedience to their religious heritage; they are quietly called to this encounter by a deep and persistent inner voice without knowing exactly why. This entry is through listening and obeying the prick of an inner demand, sometimes like a poke in the ribs, which will not let them alone unless they continue the religious journey. This way is well described in Acts 10, in the story of Cornelius, a first-century Gentile. He knew that he needed something, and he went on being faithful in his prayers and continuing his acts of charity and kindness until one day God sent an angel to prepare him to receive Peter, who came with instructions. One must never underestimate the power of this way of entry — the faithful, continuous, daily religious practice. It is often this kind of practice which brings a transforming religious encounter to set fire to our lives. But this way is still not always enough for some of us.

Some people find their way to the spiritual journey through an unlikely avenue — despair and anxiety — and this also is a legitimate way. There are some of us who have plumbed the depth of life and found it meaningless. We have worked to produce something which never quite comes off. We have taken the philosophers in stride and found that they are dust and ashes. We have experimented with physical pleasure to the point of satiety, until there is no place

27

to run. And so we turn to the one aspect of life which we have left out, God, and find the loving, forgiving Christ waiting to receive us. It was in this way that Augustine started his spiritual quest, which was to shape the course of Christian culture for centuries.

Luther's spiritual trek may well have begun in this way, and from what we know of Baron von Hügel, this was undoubtedly the beginning of his search as well. Very likely the common attitude of people toward despair and anxiety needs to be reconsidered; these conditions may for some be the unavoidable pains of spiritual rebirth, rather than just fearful symptoms of mental weakness.

There are also those sensible few who reflect enough about life to realize that all is not well with them. They set out to find some meaning, some purpose and destiny which cannot be found in the secular world, and this search leads them ultimately to the religious journey. This was apparently the way of such early Christians as Justin Martyr or Cyprian, and of some in the modern world as well.

For the first three centuries, belonging to a Christian community was incredibly dangerous, difficult, and hard. The Christian communities were illegal, and Christians faced the constant threat of persecution. If members of the community were discovered by informers and reported to the government, the consequences were catastrophic; death or slavery could result. This very danger made their constant fellowship with God and one another *necessary*. The kingdom of God was so real to them that their communities grew in spite of all the danger. We can be grateful to those who kept Christianity alive under such circumstances, and grateful that we do not face such a challenge (though Christians still face persecution in some parts of the world). No real Christian seeks persecution, but when it comes the heavens may open as they did for Stephen when he was stoned (Acts 7:54-60). *Seeking* martyrdom, however, was forbidden in the early Church. The Greek word describing the "hard" way is one that can cause catastrophic suffering.[2]

All of these approaches to the spiritual journey have one central theme in common. They all partake of a deep humility, a deep inner sense that something is lacking within the searcher, something the searcher has not found which makes him or her less than half a real human being. This humility is essential for the successful spiritual quest. Those who are perfectly adjusted to this world and completely comfortable in the "good life" can rarely be touched by God. Indeed, few of us get very far on the spiritual journey who do not have the genuine and deep inner motivation of those who can say, "Something is lacking in me which I must somehow find." The sense of a lack leads us to move continually from one level of relationship with God to another, deeper one. The journey has no end.

It should be obvious at this point that people can get into this spiritual venture for some very wrong reasons. A person who thinks merely that it looks like fun may suffer far worse than disillusionment. The spiritual world is real, and it has great heights and depths. Jumping into deep meditation without a guide and time-tested religious tradition is like putting out to sea in a small pleasure craft. Such Christian saints as John of the Cross wrote of their turbulent feelings, which they expressed through such images as ocean tides and storms; a reality this powerful can wreck a life that is not prepared for it. Equally disastrous is the attempt to slip into the spiritual journey as an escape from the responsibilities of outer physical life. The deep wisdom of Jesus and Christianity tells us that we need to be genuinely engaged with our brothers and sisters both in fellowship and in mutual support as we seek to grow in relationship with God and the kingdom of heaven. All human beings are our brothers and sisters; all have infinite value; and we must not flee from human relationships.

Neither is it good to use a particular spiritual practice just because someone else is using it. What is good for one person may poison another. In recent years a new interest has been kindled in spiritual practice both for groups and for individuals. One of the questions that is most often addressed to me is: "How do I find a spiritual director, guide, or companion?" We want to find someone who will not violate our boundaries and who is part of a deeply committed fellowship. A wise scripture verse states, "You must not move your neighbor's boundary marker" (Dt 19:15). This statement has often been called the eleventh commandment, and it is just as valid for our inner boundaries as for our homestead in the physical world.

The genuine religious quest, then, is marked by a serious searching and so by a deep humility; it is never an offhand or frivolous undertaking. Those who embark on this quest are exploring their need for the assurance and joy that are its end result. What kind of spiritual companions do we need?

Seek Out Christian Spiritual Fellowship and Guidance

We need companions on the spiritual journey, people who can help us evaluate our experience and our relationships with one another. But finding such companions is rarely easy: once we open ourselves to the spiritual journey, we may find ourselves quite alone. Few people share their most significant religious experiences. Some twenty years ago a major and careful, random-sample national survey was made of the spiritual and other uncommon experiences of the American populace. One question asked of the interviewees was: "Have you ever felt as though you were very close to a powerful, spiritual force that seemed to lift you out of yourself?"

The results were surprising. Thirty-nine percent stated they had experienced such a spiritual reality; however, when the interviewers checked back on the people who answered that question positively, they discovered that half of this group had never revealed this part of their lives to anyone prior to the survey. When questioned further, they said that the last people with whom they would have shared this information were professional religious. So it is apparent that many people fear that their experience of God will not be understood in most churches. This is why every church needs to make the effort to establish a fellowship in which our deepest religious experiences can be shared.

31

One woman who had suffered from depression told me that she had found a spiritual guide who combined the understanding of the spiritual way with a knowledge of the soul; this guide helped the woman find the road to healing. It is good to remember that the root meaning of psychology is the study of the *soul*. Real psychology always needs to take account of the religious dimension of the psyche. This woman wanted to give a large sum of money to start a program in Christian Spiritual Companionship in a Christian seminary.

The program was to prepare clergy and lay people as spiritual guides. One seminary faculty met to decide whether the money should be accepted and the program inaugurated. Their first and most serious question was: "What is spirituality?" The faculty questioned the value of such a program until one Asian faculty member spoke up: "Gentlemen, you may not know what spirituality is, but this is what our students are asking for."

Lecturing to Christian clergy in Asia, I found disbelief that the West had lost its spiritual roots. The spiritual world was just as real to them as the physical one, and they could not understand Western materialism. God and the spiritual dimension is the ultimate source of reality for most Asians.

Everyone who is serious about relating to God and embarking on the spiritual journey needs to find a spiritual companion or guide and a group with whom to share. It should be noted that all the saints had their confessors, and those in monasteries their directors of conscience. Those who have been the most serious and have gone the farthest on the religious journey have all sought and found such invaluable help. Simply the fact of seeking such direction contributes much to one's humility, because it is an outer demonstration of one's inner deficiencies. The one warning which I must give is to use care in the selection of a spiritual guide or group. Only those who are on a spiritual pilgrimage themselves can safely help or guide others. The blind cannot lead the blind without falling into one pit or another.

If we can find no one who has been specifically trained, we at least need a spiritual friend with whom we can speak of the deeper and more mysterious experiences which come to most of us as we move further on the spiritual journey. I have known of no one following the spiritual way who has not been grateful for another who will listen as we talk about our most sacred experiences. A group can begin with two. Most of us keep our spiritual experiences concealed for fear of being misunderstood and mocked. However, those who are sensitive and keep their eyes and ears open usually find others like themselves.

Many years ago I was serving a large church. I attended a weekday eucharist every week, and I noted that several people came early to the service and lingered afterward. We discovered we all wanted to grow in the spiritual life. We found we could share our insights and books; we could pray together and support one another. Through this group my wife and I met some of the most spirit-filled people we have ever known.

The story is told of an Indian guru (I would not prescribe the action described in the story, but it still makes an important point). A man sought out a guru and asked him to show him how to find God. The holy man looked incredulously at the pilgrim and asked several times if he were really in earnest. Each time the man protested, "Yes, yes! There is nothing in the world I want more than to find God." Finally the old teacher strode out into the Ganges with the seeker and looked him sternly in the eye. "Are you sure? Do you really want to find God?" he asked. "Oh, yes!" came the answer, and the teacher plunged the man's head under the water and held him there until the last bubble of air came from his hapless lips. Then the guru let him come up, gasping for breath. "And what do you want now, more than anything else?" the guru asked. "Oh! for a breath of air!" the man gasped. And the guru answered dryly, "When you want God that much, you will find him." This is how much a seeker needs to find God — but there are enough problems in life to lead us to God without the guru's dramatic approach.

Spiritual companions, like God, are found when the need is there. It may cost time, or money, or travel, but they can be found. Among the particular instances which I recall, one happened several years ago in an isolated university town where neither religious nor psychological guidance or fellowship of this kind was available. A friend teaching there, who was searching and in deep need at the time, joined with her associates to find a new approach in their work with children and the correction for certain of their problems. This group studied religious and other approaches. They concluded that they must first come to know themselves, and so, without any do-it-yourself text, they began to share deeply with each other and then to act as spiritual companions for each other. By sharing deep personal insights and experiences, and by also studying together, these individuals came into an amazing contact with the world of spirit which continued through the years. Besides developing new techniques in their field which have since become widely accepted, they continued to see the results in their own lives and in the lives of others. Many people have my friend to thank because she realized the need for spiritual fellowship and did something about it.

The importance of knowing our need for something more than what we have cannot be stressed enough. God responds to seekers.

Finding Spiritual Companions

There is an increasing openness and hunger for spiritual fellowship in the Western world. When it is not available in our traditional churches, many people look elsewhere. Of course most of the great religions have group services and individual spiritual practices, which have been tested by time and can offer valuable insights into the spiritual life. But no religion has the richness and depth or unique spirituality that is found in Christianity. We need to be cautious in following any spiritual guide or group which offers a spiritual path that has not been tested by time. We also need to beware of any practice that springs out of one person's experience and is taught as the final truth. Real Christian spiritual fellowship is a five-pointed star. Let me describe its five "points."

First of all, Christian spirituality is rooted in more

than three thousand years of Jewish and Christian history and tradition. The Bible, Christian scripture, is a library of books going back to the dawn of human writing. In order to interpret this treasure house of spiritual insight, we need an interpreter. God has given us his Son to live out in history the essence of God's love for us. And so Jesus came among us, lived and loved, taught and died and rose again. His spirit is still among us and within us forever, sublime and homely, rich and simple, divinely above us and divinely near.[1] Jesus is our interpreter, our individual and communal guide.

We need more than just tradition, however. Tradition alone can be like dead leaves in a fall rain. Carlo Carretto of the Little Brothers of Jesus wrote, "Jesus came to bring us fire and not a catechism."[2] We need a relationship with Jesus, not just an intellectual knowledge of the Bible or Church history or theology or the outer events in the life of Christ. Tradition is important and we need to check our experiences with our spiritual foundations, but we need to supplement such intellectual foundations with rich personal experience.

A new sense of openness to the Holy Spirit developed in the protestant Church with the charismatic renewal. Then Pope John XXIII called on the Roman Catholic Church to pray for the outpouring of the Spirit. This led to the revolutionary Second Vatican Council, in which Leon-Joseph Cardinal Suenens played a significant role. This intellectual and spiritual giant said to me one day when we were walking in a garden, "I never feel any more like a child of God than when I am speaking in tongues." Not all of us receive the gift of tongues, however; the Spirit of God has various ways of relating to us human beings. We always need to be open to the many ways the Spirit speaks.

Those of us who wish to walk with others on the spiritual journey need to know the history and tradition of our scripture and Church. The Bible is in essence a record of the religious experiences of the people of God. We need to know and be open to the tremendous variety of spiritual experiences, ways that God communicates with us. Knowing this history and tradition helps to keep us on track. Then we need to experience for ourselves the spirit of the risen Jesus, which gives us the wisdom to know our specific pathway on the spiritual pilgrimage. These are the first two points of the five-pointed star.

The third element of genuine spirituality is the conviction that our physical world is surrounded and penetrated by the reality of God and the kingdom of heaven. People can be psychologically depressed because they have been cut off from their religious roots, brainwashed by secular society. Many in the West have been taught to believe that humanity is part of a purely mechanical, meaningless world; hence, their minds tell them that what their hearts believe is nonsense. One reason for the dramatic growth of the Christian Church in Korea and Singapore is that most educated people there can't imagine that sensible people could believe that the material world is all there is.

Some years ago a very well-educated clergyman came to me in despair. He felt that he was lost. He had come to realize that he did not have a view of the universe which had a place for an experience of God and the spiritual journey. As he discovered that many of the leading scientists no longer had a closed mind to religion, his faith gradually returned and his depression lifted.

A spiritual companion needs to meet people where they are. I find that I need to keep up my knowledge of science in order to know that we live in a mysterious universe. In the last fifteen years, our view of the universe and our capacity to understand it have become increasingly wonderful, and sharing this new scientific insight with others can be revelatory and healing. People who have no place for God or the spiritual in their lives and thinking may be the very people who need spiritual companions the most, particularly when they face their mortality.

Some of the finest Christians I have known were agnostics who were reached by the humble, gentle understanding of friends who acted as uncritical, caring, open, compassionate spiritual companions. Most people are better than they think. Concern and caring for them brings forth the hidden best in us. Arguing or disagreeing seldom do this. We are likely to be threatened by nonbelievers only when our own convictions about the love and kingdom of God are weak. Being companions to those caught in secular materialism is a special vocation that needs understanding and support.

As we study the varieties of religious experience, we realize that we need others to check on us. Some so-called religious practices are not healthy. Spiritual companions need to have other spiritual friends who can help them see themselves as they really are and see how they can be closer to God. Most of us want this kind of spiritual checkup if it is offered in Christian love. The fourth point of the star is our constant need for one another.

The last and most important qualification for a spiritual companion is the capacity to share the healing mercy of God with people who need it. We need the kind of love that the early Christians showed for one another under persecution. The pagans had never seen anything like this love before. They were drawn to this love because it gave meaning to their dull, aimless, power-driven lives. The star of Christian spirituality needs all five of its points if it is to shine brightly. This last qualification — the ability to share God's healing mercy — is so important that we shall look at it in much greater depth later on.[3]

Learn the Mystery of Silence

Praying to God is not only speaking to God but also listening to God. How seldom do we place ourselves in the presence of the risen Christ and then simply quiet down and listen. But this is just what we need to do: We cannot know anyone well to whom we have not listened. We can seldom share the transforming love of Christ unless we have exposed ourselves to it in silence and meditated on Jesus' life and words. Unless we detach ourselves for a time from the busyness of our everyday lives and allow ourselves to experience the love of the resurrected Jesus, we have little to share with our brothers and sisters except our own human love. In all the major religions of the world we find an emphasis on detachment.

In some of the religions of the East, we find little value placed on turning back to human attachments, but in Christianity, after we have become detached, we are again expected to turn outward to our fellow human beings and share spiritually and physically what we have and are.

Silence and detachment are not very popular in our secular society. Until we practice silence, we seldom realize the rich beauty and complexity that God has created in the human soul. We need to realize that we have been made not only to know the physical universe but also to know our holy, loving God who made that universe. We need to look beyond the limits of our material world. We can do this as we center down in silence. Even Jesus needed silence as he went up into the mountains to commune with Abba. In silence we turn away from total preoccupation with our daily busyness.

Much modern life looks like a studied attempt to avoid ever being alone and faced with the spiritual dimension of reality. We begin the day with the radio alarm clock, which connects us to a disc jockey. As we come to breakfast, we face the news bombardment. We eat our breakfast between a flow of words — headlines, politics, ads, murder trials. The radio plays as we drive to work. Pipeline music flows around us as we work, and then we attend a business luncheon, do more work, and drive home still connected to the car radio. Then we watch TV, with wars and rumors of wars, or a violent video, before falling into bed too tired to dream. If sleep does not come, there is the ever-present sleeping pill or tranquilizer to remove the necessity of a nighttime encounter with silence. And the next day the same diet of noise starts all over again.

In such lives the Spirit of God has little chance of breaking through except in sickness or old age, and then who heeds its call? This kind of living reveals more about our beliefs than anything we can say. It expresses our doubts about the value of a fellowship with God. Until we cease this all-consuming busyness, there is little chance for any sustained spiritual encounter. As long as we keep riding off in all directions at once, like the perfect English gentleman in Edward Lear's *Nonsense* story, we are not very likely to start our own inner journey or find a fellowship to guide us.

This is almost exactly the story of one clergyman who came to Jung suffering from a nervous breakdown. The story he told was a simple one, familiar to so many of us; he had been working fourteen hours a day, and his nerves were shot. Jung's instructions were quite simple. The man was to work only eight hours and then go home and spend the evening quietly in his study, all alone. Since the man was in real agony, he made up his mind to follow the prescription exactly. After he had worked his eight hours, he returned home, had his supper, told his wife his plan, and went into his study and closed the door. And there he stayed for several hours. He played a few Chopin Etudes and finished a Hermann Hesse novel. The next day was the same, except that during his time alone he read Thomas Mann and played a Mozart sonata. On the following morning he went back to see Dr. Jung who asked him how he felt.

When he complained that he was no better, Jung inquired just what he had done, and he heard the man's recital of activities. "But you didn't understand," Dr. Jung told him, "I didn't want you with Hermann Hesse or Thomas Mann, or even Mozart and Chopin. I wanted you to be all alone with yourself." At this the poor man looked terrified and exclaimed, "Oh! but I can't think of any worse company." To which Dr. Jung gave his classic reply: "And yet this is the self you have been inflicting on other people fourteen hours a day."

The result of real silence can be amazing indeed. I remember particularly the experience of one young man, not quite nineteen, who had come to me in a bad way, completely uncertain about his future. He seemed to do everything he wanted not to do and had no energy for the things he really wanted to do. I suggested that he go up to a mountain cabin for several days to get away from what had become pointless busyness. There was no one he could talk to there, and he was to do nothing and eat lightly. He went and stuck it out for thirty-six hours. This was all he could stand, but he came back on the second day with a dream that revealed the depth of himself and showed him exactly what was wrong. As a result — the direct result of his spending time alone — he was able to start off on the right path again.

My first experiences of listening in silence touched me deeply. I had just started to keep a journal. Life seemed gloomy and gray. I went into the back of the church and sat down. I just waited in the silence. I wrote down how I felt as clearly as possible. I don't remember how long I was there. And then the words came to me, "You should rejoice. Grayness means that the sun is trying to break through." Then the sun did break through and the dark clouds disappeared. I had allowed God's presence and light to penetrate through my inner fog and dissipate it. God's presence and light are always present, but we need to be open to them and let them emerge. I shared this experience with our prayer group, and it lifted the spirits of all of us. For fifty years this has been a reality I have been able to count on.

This practice of silence or quiet detachment as a religious discipline is particularly important for people who are caught up almost totally in the outer material world. But silence alone is never enough. Furthermore, a retreat to silence is not for all people at all times. For the person who is not doing enough in the outer world, who is tempted to withdraw and look only for satisfaction inwardly, the discipline of detachment can be harmful. Its purpose, of course, is an adequate relation to both the spiritual and the outer physical worlds; like most of my other suggestions, this is a general prescription which must be fitted to individuals and their own needs. Here again is an indication of how valuable it is to have other people or a group as objective friends, with whom we can discuss all facets of our spiritual lives. This is often the only way to keep from getting off on the wrong track and becoming set in it. We need to reach both upward to God and outward to other human beings, particularly to our spiritual friends.

For most of us, however, our journey to God is a practical impossibility until all outer activity has come to a halt, until we are quiet. We have to learn to be alone *and useless*, to do nothing, in order to open the door fully to God and the kingdom, to a level not directed by our conscious activity. Real progress on the spiritual road begins when we learn to be still and listen. It may be hard for some people to remember even a single day which they spent alone in this manner. Perhaps it was during an illness, for sickness does have value in that it brings our outer activity to a grinding halt.

All the masters of the devotional life prescribe silence and quiet listening as an utter necessity for spiritual growth. Fenelon even directed that we should not speak if it is possible to keep silent. The philosopher Thomas Carlyle advised: "Do thou thyself but hold thy tongue for one day: on the morrow, how much clearer are thy purposes and duties; what wreck and rubbish have these mute workmen within thee swept away, when intrusive noises were shut out!"[1]

One of Kierkegaard's most delightful passages suggests that most human beings are like a kind of social bird that promptly dies when it has to be alone. In *The Sickness unto Death*, Kierkegaard goes on to say: "In the constant sociability of our age people shudder at solitude to such a degree that they know no other use to put it to but (oh, admirable epigram!) as a punishment for criminals."[2]

Many traditions support the discipline of silence, which undoubtedly goes back at least to the commandment about keeping holy the Sabbath day. This discipline has been embodied in the submission of some Trappist monks to a life-long vow of silence and in the discovery by the Quakers that silence is the center around which they can best come into God's presence. Like the tradition of silence before and after the services in certain churches, each of these practices conveys the same truth and meaning that are also expressed by writers speaking from many non-religious points of view, for instance Anne Morrow Lindbergh in her *Gift from the Sea*. What they all agree about is that this inner life, the world of spirit, can be discovered through the practice of silence, either alone or with others. One of the most profound statements of this truth is found in John of the Cross' poetic masterpiece, *Dark Night of the Soul*.[3]

Each of us needs to discover for ourselves how long the silence need be, or how often. But first we need to find time for it. When we claim that we are just too busy to be silent, then usually we are just too busy! There are as many ways of finding the time for quiet reflection as there are hours of the day. For one friend of mine, an early hour of the active day was best, and if the telephone rang during her quiet time, she simply let the answering machine tell the caller, matter-of-factly, that she had someone with her and would call back. Other people really require the silence of the night, or a place that is free of interruptions, or a group praying together. The way we find the time for silence makes very little difference. Also, after group silence we need to make time to share any insights that have emerged out of the silence of the kingdom. For many Christians, eucharist is the best way to begin or conclude our silence together; it is a foretaste of the fellowship of heaven.

I find I need a time each day lasting from fifteen minutes to an hour. I also need a weekly time of an hour or so to collect the tattered fragments of my life, and at least once a year I need a day or two of retreat to center down and get my priorities straight — to see who I am and where I am going, to find out what God and my spiritual companions need from me. The crucial matter *is whether we do or do not find and keep a time of silence alone and with others, because this is a good measure of just how sincere we are in going forward on the spiritual journey.* Many fail to heed this signpost.

Out of this silence come stirrings which we did not know existed within us. The bridge created by holy silence opens the depth of our souls to be known; strange, hidden things come up, some of them wonderful and others shocking to discover. In the silence, when there is no one else to hold accountable, and no busyness to act as a cloak of self-deception, it is almost impossible to be dishonest. Fears and remembrances may then be stirred up which we need to be attended to or shared with a friend or a group of spiritual companions. This kind of self-discovery can lead us into the presence of God.

Here a prayer group of like-minded people can be invaluable. Two or more people can gather together in silence and share what comes out of this quiet time. Indeed, many persons find it easier to be silent with others than alone. They are not only able to become genuinely silent more quickly with others, but they create a fellowship in this way which can help all of them toward greater spiritual maturity.

As a matter of fact, it takes real discipline for even the best of us when we are alone to be silent and to turn our total attention to God and the kingdom of heaven. Teresa of Avila tells of her experience of going into the chapel to pray. As she tried to be silent and listen, she noticed that the altar cloth was not properly draped. She thought to herself: "I really should go and straighten it. But no, I am here to pray and come into the presence of God." She then tried to be silent again, and she heard some workmen repairing tile on the roof. Again her mind wandered and she thought that she should go out and supervise the job. No, she considered: "I am here to pray and praise and be fed by the presence of God." If Teresa had problems coming into the inner castle, how much more will ordinary Christians find this practice difficult? Considering the difficulty of this practice, we need to put a high priority upon our silent communion with God if we are to achieve it.

If we are going to be still, we need a time without interruptions and a place where we can be comfortable. Then, as we quiet down, we usually begin to see a flood of unrelated images and ideas — plans for the next day, tasks we have left undone, hopes we have not realized. At this point I find the use of a journal very helpful. I can jot down things I have forgotten or jobs that need to be done. I then say to myself, "I will take care of you later, but now it is time for me to become aware of the presence of the risen Christ and be fed and restored."

We cannot be quiet using violent methods, but only as we gently push aside these interrupting thoughts and concerns. Coming into real silence is like eating an artichoke . . . leaf by leaf by leaf. If I try to swallow it whole, I end up with a mouthful of thistles. Many people find the saying of the rosary a way of quieting down to experience the merciful Mother of God. Other people find that the Jesus prayer — "Jesus son of God have mercy upon me a sinner" — brings them into a quiet and meditative state. Still others simply breathe deeply and experience the Spirit of God surrounding them. As we quiet down, we may hear the still, small voice of God. The more we learn to listen to one another, the more likely we are to hear the voice of the loving God.

Loving God and our companions requires listening to them, and this takes discipline. We must learn truly to listen to one another and to God. And in order to listen, we ourselves need to be silent.

Practice the Art of Christian Contemplation

Most of us who wish to do so can learn to contemplate the mystery of our loving God who came among us as Jesus of Nazareth. When we contemplate something, we do not try to understand it or analyze it. We gaze upon it in awe. In order to contemplate, we need first to be silent; we accept the object as it is. The actual word "contemplate" comes from the Latin and means "to go into the temple to seek guidance." In contemplating our God, we open ourselves to a reality wiser and deeper than we; we listen and behold.

There are two quite different ways of knowing. In one we open ourselves to the silence within a group or as an individual and wait upon that which we wish to know. This kind of knowing is quite different from the process of rational thought, in which many of us have been almost exclusively trained. Rational thinking — directed, analytical thought, proceeding by logical reasoning from a basic concept — is probably the most characteristic tool of our present culture. It has given us our computers, as well as our philosophy and our mathematics. As this analytical power has been turned upon matter, the physical world has yielded up many of its secrets. But, as any basic scientist knows, there is another kind of thinking, a more intuitive kind, which is equally important in science and is even more important and basic to ordinary human life. Rational thinking cannot spin out the intuitions upon which science is based, and it certainly does not reveal the secrets of the spirit. This takes another kind of knowing — experiencing through pictures rather than concepts, experience which is passive rather than active, which follows a meaning that seems to be independent of the rational mind. Some of the greatest scientists, people who have created our latest communication skills, have used a passive contemplation as a means of discovery. From this kind of knowing have also come our great works of art and poetry, and it is this experience that unlocks the secret of the kingdom of God.

We need to learn this second kind of knowing if we are to discover the kingdom of heaven. In fact, it takes as much learning to grow in Christian contemplation as it does to develop rational thinking. As a culture, we have nearly forgotten how to use this power to experience contemplatively. And so we know less about how to make direct contact with God, for this contact, as Aquinas so clearly suggested, is made through contemplation. This is unquestionably one reason we have so much difficulty understanding the Bible and religious writing. We cannot think ourselves to God; we need to be open to experience what God gives, to wait upon the Holy One.

When we contemplate, we enter the silence and allow our souls to ponder, to weigh all the data. We ruminate, listen deeply. We read with our hearts and souls; we behold, gaze upon, are open to. No one word describes what our deepest relationship with God can be better than "contemplate." This wonderful word tells us how best we can read religious books.

Often we try to carry our way of rational, secular reading over to our religious reading, reading which should deepen and enrich our spiritual lives and lead us on our spiritual journey.

So much of our reading is for escape, and we read only with our heads. We tear into a book rather than letting it open its inner depth to us. It is as if we had spied some rare mountain goats and could choose whether to shoot one on the spot and tear it apart for food, or to follow them and let them lead us into their mountain fastnesses where we watch them carefully. The first kind — studied, discursive reading — fills the bill for an immediate, already well-determined hunger, but contemplative reading is quite different. It grazes and munches, slowly, selectively. Most of us, as Baron von Hügel once suggested, would die of malnutrition if we tried to be like cows in our reading. We would probably go into such a fit over each morsel we could not eat that we would obtain little value from the nourishing parts. And yet contemplative reading has to be done very much as a cow grazes, skipping through what we cannot digest and stopping to munch on the parts we can assimilate. It is a way of reading that has to be learned.

Seldom do we touch the real value of the Bible or spiritual books unless we approach them contemplatively. I remember well one friend, a very smart fellow, who felt that he ought to add reading the Bible to his many accomplishments. He read it very carefully, analytically, and when he got through he could have passed a theological school examination on Bible content. But the main thought that stayed with him from his reading was that the stories were a bit too far-fetched to have much meaning for anyone today. He had not allowed the words of the book to work as a leaven in him, and he might just as well have read the World Almanac for all the religious value he received. He did not know how to contemplate the scriptures.

There are many ways to unlock and release our powers of contemplation and meditation. We need to find which pathway is best for us.

One of the most common practices is the *lectio divina*, which was common in the Western Church for centuries, back before most people could read or write. A passage of scripture was read (*lectio*). The people present listened to it and perhaps memorized it. Then the people were called to engage with the passage. Perhaps the passage that was read was the story of Bartimaeus (Mk 10:46-52), the blind man who calls out to Jesus for the gift of sight. The *lectio divina* would have listeners reflect on what they, like Bartimaeus, truly want the most from God. Then the listeners would identify with the blind beggar who has been healed, and they write a hymn of thanksgiving that might have come from Bartimaeus' mouth. During this stage of praying called meditation (*meditatio*), practitioners of the *lectio divina* try to understand the story and its meaning for themselves.

We have a God who listens to us. We can come into the presence of the risen Christ and talk with him. And someone talks back. We can speak of our fear and unhappiness or of our joy and hope, and new insights rise up from the silence. We look around the group in which we are using this form of shared caring. We may see these people in a new light. We listen to God through the scripture and through the lives of those around us. In the *lectio divina* this level is known as prayer (*oratio*). Contemplation (*contemplatio*) is considered the final stage of the prayer journey, though I use this word more broadly to signify the wholehearted opening of ourselves to the holy, healing Christ.

In that final, contemplative stage of prayer, we simply open ourselves to receive and experience the grace we have requested. At this time we usually find new insights, which usually have a greater effect on us if we record them in our journals. We can also express our new insights in drawings or in molding clay. Finally, one of the best parts of the spiritual journey is sharing with others what we have experienced and receiving their response to our contemplation.[1] We learn much about each other as we share our new insights and listen to others share theirs. All of those in such a fellowship grow spiritually; shared prayer and contemplation make for real fellowship in which each member of the group is strengthened in the experience of God.

The Bible is the history of God's reaching out to human beings. The events come to dramatic climax in the life and death, resurrection and ascension of Jesus of Nazareth. But the account of God's work among human beings does not end there. Jesus' disciples and followers formed groups to share the transforming reality of Jesus' continued presence. They found the Bible a continuing source of courage, strength, and hope. They celebrated their eucharists (services of thanksgiving) in spite of all the persecution they endured. They experienced the living Christ as they broke bread and shared the cup. They heard the voice and message of Jesus as his parables were read at their secret gatherings. Their entire lives were contemplative and meditative; they experienced contemplative reading and living the gospel.

Let us take for example, the account of the raising of Lazarus. We are first told that Jesus was summoned because of Lazarus' illness, and he tarried in coming. When at last Jesus reached the bereaved sisters, they told their friend reproachfully, "Lord, if you had come, Lazarus would be alive." And after Jesus had spoken to them about what it meant to be truly alive, they all went to the tomb. Jesus wept and turned to the crowd of mourners and told them to take away the stone that sealed the tomb. Jesus had to insist, because they protested that the body had been buried for four days and had begun to decompose. With the tomb open, Jesus prayed a prayer of certainty and called out in a loud voice, "Lazarus, come forth!" And Lazarus came forth, still bound in his burial wrappings, and Jesus gave the people who stood there amazed a final command: "Unbind him."

Here we have a story which is historically true and is also a subject of contemplation. In spite of the fact that meditation expands our knowledge of God, let us see what can actually come from contemplating the meaning of these events. So often when we ask God to take over — whatever the guise in which we see the divine — God seems to tarry. God waits, needlessly it seems, until what is sick in us has died: Our hope, our courage, and our capacity to love may be sick unto death. And when this part of us needs to be resurrected, then we learn what it means to be alive

— on faith. While parts of us are blaming fate, we still must go to the tomb and weep over the person that is no longer alive in us and ask clearly for obstructions to be removed.

The trouble with so much religion today is that it tries to avoid the dead parts of our lives. If we avoid them, we need not weep. If we avoid them, we need not come into relationship by demanding to be helped actively. If we avoid them, we can do without the courage it takes to face the stench that goes with death. But then we also do without the transformation. Christianity is the journey of passing through defeat to eternal victory.

To come alive we have to be sorry for the dead part of ourselves, sorry enough to say what needs to be done and strong enough to face up to the evil that caused the death. We have to be sorry enough so that we want life and will pray for it. Then, with faith and certainty, we can call out in a loud voice; the dead within us comes forth, and we are ready for the final action of setting it free. Nothing is completely dead within us, so dead that it cannot be raised. And this story puts the question: What is the dead Lazarus within me? What part have I allowed to die so that I am living only as a partial human being, busy getting more and more set in my own one-sidedness? I need to remember Jesus can bring any part of us back to life.

This boundless mine of precious material is available to any of us. For instance, one might read Numbers 13 — seeing oneself as one of Moses' spies in the promised land — and begin to wonder if it is always necessary to feel like a grasshopper among giants who have "arrived." Other people might even find themselves in the Christmas story itself, perhaps first wishing they could get into the inn, and then turning to the stable with its animals and a few none-too-bright shepherds, wondering what it means that this is the place of the birth, the place where even the Magi come to bring their gifts. Indeed there is no limit to the depth of insight which can come from the Bible's pages when they are listened to with the listening soul.

When we gaze and ponder on the various resurrection appearances and then allow these events to be recreated within us, we find that some of the wonder and healing of those events begins to take place in our lives. If we are pulled up with our own goodness, we need only to wait and watch before the three crosses of Golgotha. They reveal the tainted stream of destructiveness in human life that made these crosses possible. But unfortunately, the Church has often dwelt too much on this one great tragedy, when most of us probably need more often to spend an hour with the men who brought the paralytic to be healed by Jesus or to listen in depth to one of the parables. I recommend John Sanford's *The Kingdom Within* as a book that helps a reader tap the deeper meaning of the parables of the kingdom.

This way of penetrating the depth of the Bible should be used in addition to rational study. Again, it is not a matter of *either/or,* but of using *both* practices. Contemplation provides the reason for spending effort on intellectual and critical understanding. Once we have been touched by these events, then we want the best knowledge possible of all Jesus actually said and did. But unless the events have transforming power, why bother?

At times some of us must start from the negative side of our experience, from our own darkness and trouble. Almost all of us have times when we are seized by pain and agony, and we realize that the trouble has little to do with outer causes and events. It seems to rise from within. In order to deal with this inner darkness, I find that I must allow the mood to reveal itself. But before I can do this, I need to admit the possibility that there is an evil force or reality (the Evil One) which can attack human beings. In the Lord's Prayer, Jesus tells us to pray, "Deliver us from the Evil One," and all the saints have stressed the reality of the Evil One. Indeed, the further advanced we are along the spiritual road, the more likely we are to be the victim of these attacks; when one is already fully in the hands of "his satanic majesty," attacks are not particularly necessary.

Many people who are afflicted with darkness find that wearing a cross helps greatly in calling upon the restoring and re-creative power of the Christ. There on the cross the forces of evil tried to strike down the best of humanity, God's Son. The evil forces failed. The cross is the sign of God's triumph over those forces, and a visible and tangible sign helps some of us to participate in this victory when we need it most.[2] This is not magic but the creative opening of the spiritual realm by a meditative act. In addition, individuals who are struck with darkness need fellowship to support them and give them stability; wise caring is a great defense and healer.

One of the greatest gifts that I have been given is

my wife, Barbara, my companion of more than fifty years. She observed how much my life changed as I began to use the Ignation form of prayer, which uses the kind of meditative contemplation with a religious text that I have been illustrating. She also saw as we lectured together how this form of meditative prayer helped people who were caught in the darkness of their spiritual confusion. However, this method did not work for her. She has called her own spiritual pathway contemplation — the word that I have adopted for the practice and goal of the spiritual journey.

Each one of us needs to find our most fruitful way of praying. The pathway of one person adds new depth to the pathway of another. Each of us needs to find what we can best contribute to the group that is worshiping together. We need one another to lead us up the Holy Mountain.

Eucharist is the finest expression of becoming present to God and each other. When we come together to celebrate what God gave and still gives us in Jesus' victory over death and evil, we first of all acknowledge Jesus' presence with us, and then we confess the faults and sins that Jesus has washed from us. We ask that our hearts may be opened as we listen to the miracle of God's love and sacrifice for us. Then we bring our prayers for others, our intercessions. And we greet one another with the peace of Christ. As we come to the Holy Table to receive Christ from Christ's hands, we also bring with us our beloved and those whom we carry in our hearts. And then we receive God's blessing. The eucharist is our resting place on the journey up the steep and narrow spiritual pathway.

Learn the Value of Genuine Fasting

Few people in the Western world seriously consider the spiritual value of ever denying themselves their usual quantity of food. However, along with silence and contemplation — indeed a part of the same process — is fasting. In contemplation we turn our minds and spirits away from conscious occupation with our physical world; in fasting we turn our bodies away from the physical satisfactions of food, physical pleasure, and drink. It is easy to be self-indulgent, to take everything we want in the way of food, drink, and pleasure; we take what we want whenever we want it. If we are to take the spiritual journey with Jesus, however, we will need to consider some physical self-denial.

Jesus did not say in the Sermon on the Mount "*if* you fast," but "*when* you fast" (Mt 6:16-18). He assumed that anyone who took seriously his message about the spiritual way would already be fasting. It is true, on the other hand, that Jesus was not noted for his abstinence, as were John the Baptist and his followers. Indeed, Jesus was called a wine bibber and a glutton by his enemies (Lk 7:34). The fact that we fast certainly does not mean that we cannot enjoy a good meal; a fine meal can be a work of art. But fasting can be a valuable time of reflection: We remember the poor all over the world who are going hungry and are fasting by necessity. One third of the children all over the world go to bed hungry. As we reflect, we can give thanks for what we have and pray for those who lack.

Most of those who have seriously entered upon the spiritual journey find that a period of fasting is a great aid for them. It clears the mind and heart; it gives a new understanding of our strange and hurting world. I do not know all the reasons that it is true, but many who try fasting find the practice liberating and helpful. Somehow, as the body and mind both give up the expectation of business as usual, it becomes easier for a person to enter into the reality which is not physical. Fasting also helps us to develop discipline and self-control, qualities which are highly important on the spiritual adventure. (Many people have a problem with alcohol and lose control of their ability to handle it. We can fast in drink as well as food. This could be a good place for some people to start the discipline of fasting.) Extravagant self-indulgence, which makes a one-sided person more one-sided, is one of the easiest ways to cut the spiritual quest short.

Fasting need not be heroic. It can be a simple act like leaving the sugar out of one's tea or coffee. Such a practice is saying in action: "I do not need to have all the pleasures that I usually have." This is a symbolic action. But some people prefer a more complete fast; they find that a full day's fast with only water and orange juice slows down the entire bodily function and cleanses the mind as well as the body.

Fasting, however, must be carefully tempered by the circumstances of an individual's life. Fasting is especially helpful to persons who are too much caught up by satisfaction in the physical world, but it can be quite dangerous for those who are depressed or have already separated themselves too much from outer activities. Withdrawn, sick, or depressed people can be dragged further down into their problems by fasting, as many physicians have pointed out. Before we fast, we need to discuss our plan with some wise spiritual companion who can give us spiritual guidance. Some of us, in fact, have a real need simply to express an enjoyment of outer sensations. But for most comfortable Americans, there is one excellent reason for fasting, a practical as well as a religious reason. We are the best-fed and most poorly nourished nation on earth, according to many physicians and heart specialists. Over-eating is probably responsible for as many deaths as drinking or narcotics, and those who are over-eating themselves to death are not in the best position to undertake the religious journey in this life. I doubt they are in the most favorable condition to continue on their journey into the eternal kingdom.

We need to read and meditate on the story that Jesus told of the rich man and the beggar Lazarus (Lk 16:19-31). It is notable that Jesus calls the beggar by name but does not give a name to the rich man at whose door Lazarus sits, longing for the scraps of food thrown to the dogs. And it is the beggar who is carried off to heaven. Jesus is calling on us to reject the self-indulgent materialism of the rich man and to dedicate ourselves to lowly ones like Lazarus.

Keep a Record of Our Spiritual Journey

We tend to take writing for granted. However, when the human species learned to write, they added a whole new dimension to human experience. Before the invention of writing, we had to rely on human memory, which is quite remarkable but can hold only a tiny amount of data and cannot be passed on in its totality. Without writing, history and myth merge. Writing is the foundation of civilization, and all the great religions of humankind have a written base. Indeed, nearly all human culture is based on the ability to know the past that has been recorded and saved. With this treasure house of knowledge we can move forward to new insights.

Our modern information revolution is the result of thousands of years of writing and scientific discovery. We build upon the past. In the same way our Christian spiritual growth occurs as we integrate our understanding of the Bible and the wisdom of the saints with our own experience of the Holy Spirit and the risen Christ, which we share concretely in fellowship groups and in love with one another. It is so easy to forget how much of our Christian experience is given to us from the records of the past.

Few spiritual tools have helped me more than keeping a record of new insights in a notebook. The very suggestions I have been offering in these pages come in part from forty years of recording the ups and downs of my spiritual life. I record the times that I got off the steep and narrow path and then was found by the good Shepherd, who carried me back to the sheepfold, my spiritual home. Such written records are crucial — to individuals and to the human family at large. I am deeply grateful to Jesus' followers, who recorded the history of Jesus' life and death, resurrection, and ascension. I am grateful that they recorded his stories and parables and copied the letters of Paul and other New Testament writers. How impoverished we would be spiritually if they had not recorded the story of God entering human history as Jesus of Nazareth! We can contemplate any part of this record and be enriched.

Keeping a record of our spiritual journey is a way of reflecting on the hand of God working in our lives and revealing the meaning of scripture to us. We can turn back in our journal and read how we have been lifted out of discouragement and fear again and again by the gentle hand of the risen Jesus. We should record these experiences not to impress anyone or to get them published, but because we want to be faithful to the God who listens and reaches out to us and through us.

If we do not make some record of our experiences of God and the kingdom, we may be suggesting that these experiences are not real or that we do not really believe that we are worthy of God's love and the attention. Then we are not accepting the basic message of the risen Christ: *Everyone* has infinite value — no one is expendable. Everyone *can have a spiritual life worth recording*. One of the greatest and most treasured accounts of a spiritual journey is recorded in Augustine's *Confessions*, a book that started a new kind of religious literature. As Augustine demonstrated so many years ago, sharing our spiritual insights, victories, and failures can also encourage others in our religious fellowship.

A record of my spiritual pilgrimage can also have a very practical side. I can look back and see the effect that religious experience has had upon my life, how much God has been with me. I realize that God can use me in spite of all my faults. When I reread my journal, I am amazed at how much I have changed and how minor a seemingly insuperable problem of another time has become. Or I see that one problem persists, showing my ongoing need for God's healing power *and* showing my own ongoing effort and understanding. And there are also new insights waiting which I had not understood before, but which now turn a floodlight of meaning on my spiritual life. Biblical passages burst with new life.

Simply writing this kind of record makes our religious life more valuable. A process of clarifying goes on when in the silence we write down the concerns which seem to overwhelm us; just in the act of writing we are often able to stop "squirrel caging" and to see things in perspective again. This kind of writing keeps us close to the reality of the kingdom and helps to protect us from finding ourselves on an ego trip rather than on a real spiritual journey. When we write down our spiritual experience on paper, we can look at it objectively and see how it fits into our spiritual journey.

If we feel that we are lost on an isolated mountain top, for instance, a record of the experience can help us find a way down. Or again, if reflection shows us that we actually look on ourselves as grasshoppers up against a world of giants, then this image is far easier to handle when it is tied down in writing. Our "grasshopper complex" can lead us to transformation when it is looked at objectively and can be discussed with a friend or spiritual director or with our spiritual fellowship (Nm 13:33).

Another value in keeping a journal is surprising. The more serious attention we pay to the kingdom of God working within us, carefully recording the insights and the grace that come, the more significant and valuable is the material we are given — the more we are led and fed. The Holy Spirit responds to our concern; the Spirit's secrets are most often revealed to those who pay attention to God. The lives of those who have traveled far on this journey with the Holy Spirit bear witness to this truth. Almost every great spiritual leader has used some instrument, such as the kind of journal I am describing, to help trace out and understand the insights they have been given. Tools such as this are indispensable, and for many of us a record of our journey is unquestionably one of the best ways to make our spiritual endeavor concrete. Dated entries in our record also tell us quite vividly how often we have spent time in this kind of reflecting.

In a world that seldom takes the spiritual journey seriously, the discipline of keeping an account of our journey up the difficult path is a demonstration of our conviction that such a spiritual journey is essential to our lives. Many people have told me that the most valuable suggestion I ever made to them was to keep this day-by-day dated account of their spiritual lives. The journal can be a sacrament of our soul's spiritual journey.

God can speak to us in many different ways, and we need to be open to them. Throughout the Bible and the lives of the saints, God is continually reaching out to humans. Through images and contemplation, through visions of the night or voices which speak within us, or even in our dreams, God calls to us saying: I love you.

Abraham was called to the promised land by a dream. Joseph, the great dreamer who saved his father and brothers, said that the God who gives the dream could also interpret the dream. Samuel heard the voice of God calling him. Paul was led by his vision of the night at Troas to bring Christianity to Europe. Saint John Bosco was led by dreams in his great missionary work, and he was ordered by his Pope to record his dreams. Not all dreams are the voice of God, but God can speak through them; dreams need to be seen against the background of the Bible and Christian tradition and of our Christian fellowship. However, unless we keep a record of our inner life, we will remember only a few dreams, since most dreams are quickly forgotten.[1]

Our souls are much more wonderful than we usually realize, and God is closer to us than breath or life or thought. God wants our attention and wants to reveal our path to us. Should we not record what is given and reflect upon the divine message?

Be Honest with Ourselves and Recognize Our Mistakes

Utter honesty is a prerequisite for those making the spiritual pilgrimage, for those looking for spiritual growth and transformation. Knowing themselves and bringing all of themselves to God is a necessity for those entering the narrow gate and climbing the steep and sometimes arduous spiritual pathway. We cannot play games with the God who created us and knows us better than we know ourselves. And still God loves us more than we can imagine, loves us just as we are. The Holy Spirit wishes to bring all of us human beings into the transforming light of the kingdom. The light of the kingdom, like the light of the sun, brings growth and creativity. God wants all of us to grow to our spiritual potential — not just to remain fragments of our total selves.

Some people fail to make much progress on the spiritual journey because they do not know themselves and so hide some of the most important but seemingly least attractive parts of their total selves with a mask. The people do not advance far into the kingdom because they touch it with only one or two facets of their total selves. We tend to forget such disconcerting parts of ourselves unless we write them down.

God can hardly transform us by the spirit if we do not willingly present the parts of us that most need transformation: our anger and fears, our critical and gossipy side, our covetousness, our dishonesty, our sensual desires. God is infinitely polite and seldom breaks into the hidden dark corners of our soul until we throw open the door to our soul room and look honestly at the less pleasant parts of our selves. It is up to us to bring all of what we are, like it or not, to God and the kingdom; this requires that we know who we really are. Few of us seek to examine our flaws and to bear *all* of ourselves — including all that lies hidden within us. But to be truly creative, we must enter the narrow gate and take stock of our problems so we know how to avoid the pits that line the steep, narrow and difficult pathway. Christians believe that such self-examination is always ultimately positive, since God loves us just as we are and will help us become what we are capable of becoming.

The Bible places a great emphasis on honesty, on knowing and speaking the truth. In the Old Testament we are told not to take the Lord's name in vain: When we swear by God's name we are bound to speak the truth. Jesus goes even further and tells us that we should not have to swear by God's name. Any word we utter should be the truth. I find that as I grow in the kingdom, I learn a great deal about myself. As I meet with my brothers and sisters and listen to them and respond to them, I discover more and more about myself. It is probably impossible, however, to know all about myself and my motives unless I interact in a Christian fellowship and reflect in God's presence. Such a context helps me grow into greater and greater self-honesty — the source from which outer honesty and truth flow naturally. It is very difficult to be honest with others until we are trying to be honest with ourselves. It can take a lifetime to be entirely honest with ourselves.

I have seen many people with their masks down, and I have never yet seen any human being whose natural face was not infinitely more attractive and beautiful unmasked than masked. The ugliness we often see in the naked soul is far more than made up by its native beauty, which is more wonderful and attractive than that of any other of God's creations. When people finally open up the depth of themselves, I cannot help but love what I see. God loves us in the same way. When we come before our Creator in utter honesty, nakedly ourselves, there is a response on the part of God which opens channels of contact between God and human beings. This is the truth which C. S. Lewis told with bold power in his magnificent novel *'Til We Have Faces*.

When I am discouraged with the state of my soul and wonder how God can put up with me, I am always heartened by the transparent honesty of Paul at the end of Romans 7. There he cries out: "The good which I want to do, I fail to do; but what I do is the wrong which is against my will . . . miserable creature that I am, who is there to rescue me out of this body doomed to death?" (Rom 7:19 and 24, *New English Bible*). If God through Christ accepted Paul, he can accept us too! God longs for us to be honest with ourselves and with God; this allows God to respond to us and transform us. Private confession or confession shared with others is spiritual honesty in action. Confession and forgiveness is one of our greatest helps on the spiritual journey.

A spiritual director or a loving fellowship are both

essential in the pursuit of inner honesty as we travel toward spiritual wholeness. It is so easy for us to deceive ourselves; our closeness to ourselves and our blindness hide our most obvious faults from our own eyes. Spiritual friends who accept themselves as they are can help us to face our failings honestly without poking too hard our areas of sensitivity, which can be like a sore appendix. Such self-aware friends do not have to hide from themselves, so they can be matter-of-fact, and neither gingerly nor destructively they can help us see the distasteful parts of ourselves. Such revelations as Peter's on the rooftop at Joppa can force inner honesty in a ruthless way, but truly God-given revelations — while picturing us as we really are — never reveal more of ourselves to us than we are able to bear. We need to listen to God, to our prayer companions, and to our fellowship. Whatever helps us to come to an inner integrity, an inner honesty, also helps us along the spiritual journey.

Love Others As Christ Has Loved Us

Many of the suggestions I have been offering for spiritual growth are common to all of the great religions of humankind. However, Jesus Christ placed a unique emphasis on God's love for us human beings (imperfect as we are) and then stated bluntly that we have missed the narrow gate and the hard and stony path if we do not love one another as God has loved and continues to love us. God's love for us in Christ is mind-boggling. How many times do we need to be reminded that each and every human being is priceless? Jesus cared infinitely about our hunger and pain, and also about our growth into God's eternal kingdom.

Religions or spiritualities that place value only on the *spiritual journey* can fail to deal with human misery. On the other hand, when we try to take care only of people's social and physical problems without offering an eternal perspective, we fail to address the spiritual depth and need of the human soul. In either case we deal with only half of our humanness and leave people in a dead-end street. Prayer and quiet lead us *inward* to experience the unmerited love of Jesus. Acts of charity and mercy and love lead us *outward* to share Christ's love with others. One of Christianity's cardinal principles is this: What we have received freely, we need to share freely — both spiritually and physically.

One of Catherine of Siena's nuns wrote to her asking how she might adequately thank God for

God's unbounded mercy and love to her. Catherine replied that she would not accomplish her goal by more prayer or greater penance or by building the most magnificent church in the world; rather, this nun could show her gratitude to God by finding someone as totally unworthy of her love as she herself had been of God's love, and by pouring mercy and love and caring upon that person as Christ had poured them out on her. But if this compassion was to be real, it would need to flow from all of her, not just from the glittering image that people often present to the world.

Baron von Hügel states the same truth in another way and makes it quite concrete. Our spiritual task, von Hügel says, is to find and love the unlovable person even as God has found and loved us, and so enable this person to become lovable! Whenever and wherever Christianity has been vital, alive, and creative, we find God's love pouring out from Christians in action and practice. Sharing God's love with other human beings (both outwardly and spiritually) is one of the most significant ways in which we can express our gratitude. Like humility, gratitude is one signpost on the spiritual pilgrimage.

The importance of love is central to the teaching of Christ and is even more present in his life and suffering and in the glory of his resurrection. In Paul's writing, the word *love* may be substituted for *Holy Spirit* with almost no change in meaning; indeed, love is the action which most nearly characterizes the Holy Spirit. In 1 Peter 4:8 we find these words: "Love shall cover a multitude of sins." Love can even *cancel* faults and sins. And John wrote that those who do not love their brothers and sisters cannot love God (1 John 5:7-13). For nearly two thousand years, when men and women have lived the kind of love we are describing, they have been called saints. Christian love and saintliness are nearly synonymous.

Those who would enter the kingdom of God — the kingdom of self-giving, forgiving love — need to allow the Holy Spirit to shape their lives so that they care for others as Christ has cared for them. As we approach the door into the kingdom of love, we are given a blank key that can unlock that door. By our caring and love for others, we shape that key. Eventually the key fits the lock and the door flies open.

We cannot shape that key by our minds or "spiritual" practices alone. We may try to be spiritual and receive wonderful experiences, startling and real, but unless our caring for others flows through our spirituality, we can be cut off from the Holy Spirit. Spirituality that is not loving to the core is not Christian spirituality. Our spiritual efforts alone do not open the door to the kingdom.

When our efforts to become spiritual, to make the spiritual journey, are not integrated with love, we are in real danger. If we try to grow spiritually but we are infected with hatred, we can become agents of the ego — the dark and destructive aspects of the human soul and society. When our spiritual journey is not directed and motivated by loving concern for *all* other human beings, then we can be taken over by the negative and wrathful side of human nature and become its tool. (In his novel *Shadows of Ecstasy*, Charles Wiliams portrays this truth.) We need not look deep in ourselves or in the world around us to

73

see how many humans are directed by power (ego) or violent destructiveness. Evil has its own attractiveness, and it has caused as much chaos and death in our own century as at any time in history.

Those who genuinely express self-giving love may have little sense of experiencing the kingdom of heaven. They may have no ecstatic experiences and may even think that their lives are humdrum and dull. Yet these very humble followers of Christ may be very close to the kingdom: They may be living the essence and centrality of the spiritual pilgrimage. Those who talk much about their spiritual journey and do not reach out to others in need are deceiving themselves.

It is not necessary to be conscious of God's ecstatic presence to be instruments of God's incredible love. There are many like Saint Martin, whose way of simple kindness and concern was rewarded by the presence of Christ. Martin cut his cloak in two in order to share it with a beggar. Later in a dream-vision, Christ appeared to Martin wearing the part of the cloak that Martin had shared with the beggar. There may be some very surprised saints, who like Martin have followed a way that does not appear very "spiritual" and yet that fulfills the demands of love. Like God, love is not limited to one variety of expression.

Our need to love others in a concrete way makes several claims on us. First of all, those of us who are on the spiritual journey can no longer live entirely for ourselves; we need to become involved in the world. This does not mean taking all the world's problems into our hearts: Such a load would destroy any of us. Rather, we need, as the Quakers put it, to find our specific *concern*, some kind of social action. This is requisite if our spiritual journey is to reach its goal. When Evelyn Underhill came to Baron von Hügel (the great authority on mysticism) for direction on how to overcome her spiritual dryness, von Hügel gave her two suggestions: She was first of all to relax her strenuous prayer practice, and secondly go twice a week to work in the soup kitchens in the slums of London. How well we move forward on the spiritual journey depends on the sincerity and integrity with which we turn outward to share spiritually *and* materially. We may start on the spiritual path and find the richest experiences within it, receiving power which is startling and real, but then we may be cut off from that life and power if we fail to turn with love out toward individuals in the hurting, hungry world.

Then there is the opposite problem of falling into the brand of social action often called "do-goodism." Sincere people were disillusioned in the 1950s, and they engaged in social action. But many of them were motivated by ego — their efforts were not undergirded by a spiritual journey or divine inspiration. Helping others with their problems can become such an obsession that there is no time left for spiritual practice, for seeking the kingdom. The surest test of such onesidedness comes when our service begins to make us irritable with our families and co-workers. One student friend nearly thirty years ago went on a freedom march and landed in jail; alone in the cell he felt red-hot wrath bubble up within him. He realized that his motives were all wrong. He saw that no one could lead people to Christ without first experiencing the genuine presence of Christ, and he realized that he still had a long way to go. We need to participate in *both* social action *and* the spiritual journey. Either one alone is not enough.

Genuine Christian love makes another demand on us. We need to learn to listen to one another. Indeed, no one can truly love me in my need unless this person listens to me. In most of our society listening is a forgotten art, but listening can be learned once we realize its value. By listening, I mean emptying myself of all my thoughts, desires, and preconceptions and welcoming the totality of the other person — responding to all that another wishes to share with all of me that I know. As I discover the totality of another human soul before me, I also come to know the Spirit of God who dwells and moves in the depth of the other soul. By listening, we can truly experience the Holy through another soul. We try to listen to each person as Christ listens to us.

A fine statement of the necessity of listening for our spiritual growth comes from Rudolph Steiner: "Only to those who, by selfless listening, training themselves to be really recipient from within, in stillness, unmoved by personal opinion or feeling, only to such can the higher beings speak. . . . As long as one hurls any personal opinion or feeling against the speaker to whom one must listen, the beings of the spiritual world remain silent."[1] Even more important, there is a significant difference between listening with indifference and listening with compassionate caring, with real love; the person who wants to be heard can recognize that difference.

Some years ago a man who was not a member of my church called the church office and made an appointment to see me. We greeted each other at the door of my office, and then we sat down in chairs facing each other. I was relaxed, with my arms stretched out toward him on the arms of my chair. I waited for him to speak. Five minutes ticked by, then ten, then forty minutes. When the hour was over, he got up, came over to me, took my hand in his and said: "You will never know what this hour has meant to me. I didn't think any human being could stand my presence for an hour without words." With this statement of profound gratitude he left. Like this man, most of us long to be listened to — even if no audible words are spoken — and accepted just as we are.

This kind of listening is not easy; it must be learned, and even then it is one of the most exhausting activities a person can undertake, demanding the total soul and mind. But it is a deeply rewarding activity. Actually, I have found out more about God through the people who have come to talk with me than from any other practice. In this kind of listening, we do not try to make over the other person into what they or we think they should be; rather, we embrace another soul, and we share in the spiritual journey in which the other is engaged.

Another necessary part of practicing love is involvement in a Christian *fellowship* or *community*. These two words have been so overused that they have come to mean a superficial kind of human relating, almost a game of keeping up pretenses. Real fellowship, however, is anything but this. In genuine fellowship with other people in a small group (and two is merely the smallest group), there is an interaction of one total person with others, without the need of pretenses or masks, in an atmosphere of acceptance and love. And, in return, acceptance and love grow out of the interaction. If this kind of give and take between real people is to be possible, rather than the meeting of masks that occurs in most groups, we must know that we can safely let down our masks. But before we feel comfortable revealing what we consider are the less attractive aspects of ourselves, we must know that we will be accepted *without judgment* and will not be put on display, that we can be loved just as we are.

In order for people to share in a group, they must know that what they share will be known only to the members of the group. If small groups are to be transforming and renewing, there must be an agreement that all that is shared will be kept as confidential information within the group. This confidentiality will have no time limit. I cannot sufficiently stress the importance of this aspect of a spiritual community.

When a group of human beings meets in confidence and honesty, there will sometimes be conflict and disagreement. One of the purposes of such groups is to resolve and understand the friction and conflict that lie below the surface. Jesus never suggested that there should be no conflict among his followers — only no *unresolved* conflict. Paul did not write that we should have no anger, but that we should never let the sun go down upon the anger we have (Eph 4:26). People who run their lives so that they avoid all disagreement with others may also avoid real relationships and genuine love and fellowship. Those who are always trying to please others do not make contact with other people. Love grows from action, not from ideas and thoughts, and action involves concrete — sometimes conflictual — contact and relationship. It brings us up short to remember John's statement that we cannot truly love God until we love our neighbors, just as they are. Love is fulfilled in concrete caring for specific individuals, particularly unlovable ones.

Churches ought to be the places where we find real fellowship and relationship; yet for most people churches are the last places where they expect to find such fellowship — or to give it. Often the real person is revealed far more in the meat market and the beauty shop than in churches. In church we usually try to be what we think we ought to be, and the other people do the same, so we fail to make contact with real people. There are a few churches, however, which have begun to experiment with small groups that meet to study and discuss the basic issues of the Christian faith and to explore ways people can serve those who need them. This kind of encounter with other human beings brings about real relationship as these people meet week after week; real love begins to grow. The source of the transforming power and spirit of Methodism was in such dedicated small groups. What John and Charles Wesley did for eighteenth-century England and the United States, Chiara Lubich has done for our time, both in her writing and in her founding of the Focolare Movement.

Christian love and spiritual practice are so closely intertwined that we cannot speak meaningfully about one without referring to the other as well. Paul calls love the greatest gift that human beings can receive. What I have written here is but a brief sketch of the way love is the heart and center of the message and life of Jesus, the Christ.[2] It is not easy to follow Jesus Christ. The path is sometimes very difficult, but it is fully worth the courage and persistence that it takes.

The Goal

If love is our goal, we have failed until the Christian community is united. This is the vision of Chiara Lubich in her book, *May They All Be One*. Not only has she written powerfully urging this goal, but she has also brought together world leaders of different church bodies. Love must eventually make us one so the message of Jesus covers the earth as the waters cover the seas.[3]

Gird Yourself with
Persistence and Courage

The journey into the world of the spirit requires great persistence and courage. It is a lifetime work. If our quest is peripheral and spasmodic, we will not go far on the spiritual pilgrimage. The devotion of atomic physicists puts the spiritual quest of most religious people to shame. In order to unlock the secrets hidden in matter, these students spend a third of a lifetime in preparation, and then settle down to endless days of work and thought. The development of the computer chip has required the same kind of persistence. How often do we find people spending this kind of time and preparation, this expenditure of energy, on the spiritual journey? Wherever we find this kind of religious devotion, we can see God working in many different ways, and we see the spiritual journey bearing fruit. Many of Jesus' followers were fishermen, so they knew the necessity of persistence if they were to make a catch.

Most of us want to reach up to a shelf and take our spiritual maturity down in a package. We want to have one religious experience, one encounter with the divine, and right off the bat become oracles of divine wisdom and fountains of grace. But the effective spiritual life is not given in this way; it grows slowly. God can and does give spiritual and mental healing, revelations and visions, dreams and ecstatic experiences, but the mature religious personality is not given as a gift all at once. It grows slowly, tended and aided by God and the powers of heaven. Real spirituality grows like a redwood tree, for thousands of years — and from a tiny seed.[1] We human beings have even greater growth potential than the forest giant. It is this kind of spiritual maturity that alone provides the power to heal human relations, to cleanse hearts and minds, and to liberate souls. We saw this power at work when Mandela could forgive those who imprisoned him for nineteen years and bring peace to South Africa.

The Bible is our handbook for prayer. God called Abraham and started a new nation. Later God called Samuel. Then God sent Jesus among us to teach us and save us by his death and rising, and God surrounds us with his Holy Spirit and leads us into eternal life. Our God has given us three ways to pray: through the Creator God; through Jesus, the loving Redeemer; and through the Holy Spirit who surrounds us and supports us. We need all these ways of praying.

We need to look twice at anyone who offers us a new spiritual practice founded on powers and insights which have come suddenly as a gift to one person. Such "prophets" may well be deceiving themselves. The forces of destructiveness can turn out superb counterfeits of spirituality in just this way. Christians need to be able to distinguish between the true commodity, the mystery of the Trinity — Creator, Redeemer, and Holy Spirit — and the imitations. Historical churches, even though differing in some details, provide us with excellent guidelines when we take the time to know them and follow them.

The life of Paul is an example in point. He had a transforming and terrifying experience on the Damascus road and another at the hands of Ananias. Undoubtedly he was given the Holy Spirit, but when he tried to preach in Damascus, he had to flee for his life. This was not just because Saul the persecutor was still hated; rather, it was because Paul was not ready. Ten years of preparation and integration of his experience were necessary before Barnabas saw that Paul was prepared to guide others on the spiritual pathway (Acts 9:1-30).

Most of us, however, are in too much of a hurry to find the final truth; we think we can know the essence and heart of reality more easily than the physical scientist can learn to know one small fragment of it. Yet the same quiet, continuous persistence, so essential to science, is the only way to a significant and fruitful journey into the realm of the spirit. Patience and perseverance make saints of ordinary, fallible human beings.

Many people drop out from the spiritual journey because they do not have enough courage. They follow all the rest of the guidelines we have suggested, but when the going gets difficult, they cannot bear the suffering which is involved.

Joining together the animal and the angel within each of us is painful. Neither one can stand the other. As we bring the totality of what we are before the realm of the spirit, we begin to know real guilt. Only those who have experienced this can know how painful it is to get a clear picture of our own beastliness, egotism, cruelty, and hate — those destructive qualities. We usually attribute these nasty qualities to "bad guys," to those in slums or to other countries. It is like a bad dream to find them in ourselves, and added to this is the realization that, try as hard as we may, we never finish the task of achieving complete spiritual integration, joining the realm of the spirit with the realm of the flesh within ourselves. We often fall back into unconsciousness, and then there is shame and guilt again. Those who set out on the spiritual quest will probably suffer the gnawing pain of their own inadequacy, and this takes courage. Many of us turn away from true life and turn to rigid fundamentalism or to hopelessness and fear. We forget that courage is not the absence of fear, but the determination to press on in spite of our fear. Often we retreat because we are afraid of ourselves. Spiritual growth forces us to face and bear what we are.

The cross stands at the center of the Christian faith. If we follow the pathway of Jesus, we will eventually need to face crosses and suffering. All the saints spoke of this truth and of their sinfulness. Crosses are popular to hang around our necks, but we seldom wish to bear them in our hearts. But those who are not willing to bear the crosses in their own hearts will seldom see or be able to bear the pain and misery of others. Paul Tournier's book *Creative Suffering*, written after the death of his wife, sustained me when my son was dying. Painful as it was, the suffering surrounding my son's death spurred me to look ahead to the kingdom of heaven and a new adventure. We human beings are mortal, but we are promised something better at the end of the narrow path.

Those who are not willing to bear suffering seldom travel very far on the spiritual journey; this is difficult to understand, but it seems to be true. In his book *Through the Valley of the Kwai*, Ernest Gordon tells a true and striking story of the power of suffering to transform courageous human beings. The events took place during World War II in Southeast Asia. Through suffering in a horrible prison camp, a group of self-satisfied, complacent young men were stripped of their conceit, their egotism, their agnosticism. While enslaved in the jungles of Burma, they realized their need for God. Crushed and broken in spirit and open to God, they were touched by the power and reality of God and were transformed.

Suffering can effect spiritual transformation. But we are *never* to seek out unnecessary suffering or inflict it on other people for *their good*. We need to remember: When we seek suffering, it is masochism. When we rise above the suffering that life brings us, this is heroic victory, a new freedom. Christ and the early Church are our examples of this freedom and victory.

Give Generously of Your Material Possessions

In the Roman city of Caesarea, an amazing event took place, which changed the entire vision of the early Church. Not all of the soldiers stationed at Caesarea looked down on the Jews over whom they watched. Indeed, Cornelius, a centurion in charge of the Italian Cohort, greatly admired the Jewish people and was attracted to the moral integrity of their religion and to the Jews' deep spirituality and sense of fellowship. His admiration led him to worship with them in their synagogue where he was warmly welcomed. Cornelius also recognized how poor the Jews were. Not only did he contribute to the upkeep of the synagogue, but he also gave generous alms to those in need. He was one of the God-fearers who found a more congenial relationship with these Jews than with the professional soldiers under his command. In addition, he was a devout man who said his prayers regularly. So far he knew nothing of Jesus the Christ, but the Holy Spirit needed generous people like Cornelius to spread the good news of Jesus if that good news was to move out into the Gentile world.

One afternoon at about three o'clock, Cornelius had a vision in which he saw an angel of God, who told him that his prayers and alms had come before God. The angel told him to send messengers to Joppa to find a man named Simon Peter, and to bring this man back to Caesarea to share God's great good news. After Cornelius recovered from his fright, the angel disappeared; Cornelius recovered his equilibrium and sent off trusted servants to find Simon Peter, who was lodging with Simon, a tanner, in a house by the seaside.

God prepared Simon Peter, who had never even eaten Gentile food in a Gentile house, by sending him a dream vision telling him to go back with the people that Cornelius had sent. Living with Gentiles would have been unthinkable for Peter prior to his vision. A large group of pagans had gathered at Cornelius' house, and Simon Peter spoke to them eloquently about Jesus' resurrection. The gift of the Holy Spirit fell upon them, and many Gentiles were baptized in the name of Jesus Christ. The gap between Gentiles and Jews was bridged.

Peter saw that his message was for Jews *and* Gentiles. Even the elders in Jerusalem came to agree that the message of the risen Christ was for Gentiles as well as Jews. They had already supported the same idea for the churches that Paul had founded. All human beings were one.

Why did the Holy Spirit pick and use Cornelius? He had three essential virtues. First of all, he was a man who prayed sincerely and constantly; second, he knew God could speak even to a Gentile and that God loved him. His third virtue was that he listened to and loved the people among whom he was stationed. He appreciated these Jews and saw the beauty and depth of their religion. He worshipped with these people; he never lorded it over them. Judaism was the finest religion Cornelius had ever encountered, and he understood that the religious message Peter preached was the flowering of Judaism.

Even in his position, Cornelius cared for the Jewish people and was always fair and just. His love was expressed not only with words but with generous gifts both to the poor of the Jewish community and to the synagogue that had taught him so much. Jesus had praised the poor widow who put her last copper coin into the Temple treasury, and Cornelius showed similar generosity. The actions of Cornelius show that any generous person, even a pagan, can be a vital instrument in the mission of Jesus and the Church. Generous giving to those in need brings one close to God. It is love in action.

It is impossible to continue on the narrow and rocky spiritual pathway unless we give of our material substance for spiritual and charitable purposes. It is nonsense to say that we want to go further up the spiritual pathway, that we are giving our lives utterly to God, if we spend most of our energy and financial resources on ourselves, our desires and interests. This attitude is worse than nonsense: It is hypocrisy, and Jesus made clear what he felt about hypocrisy. When we live totally for ourselves, the spiritual path winds up in a dead-end canyon. When we come to that point, there is often a flash of lightning that illumines the whole sky and calls us to reflect.

Money is the congealed energy of our lives, what the world gives us for what it thinks we are worth — though not what God thinks we are worth. Unless we give of our money or energy for outer spiritual purposes — to individuals and institutions that are dedicated to the realm of the spirit — the spiritual journey can come to a jarring halt. Even if we do everything else I have suggested, if we avoid this outer commitment to give, we may lose our way on the spiritual journey. Giving is closely related to spirituality, and those who have little money to give can still give prayers and caring.

If we will read our Bibles carefully, we will find a strong emphasis on giving — from the story of Jacob, who vowed to give a tenth of his property to God if he returned home safely, to that of Paul, urging his church to share with one another and support the fellowship in Jerusalem. And at the center of the Christian message is God giving of himself through his Son on the cross to save all humankind. How can we ever give enough to show our gratitude for that kind of generous, sacrificial love?

One of the factors which was responsible for my deep interest in the spiritual life was my own practice of giving. Many years ago, when I had been a minister for only a few years, I heard a speaker at a clergy conference state that it is wicked to tithe. At first this seemed to be just what I was waiting to hear, because I was feeling uneasy about the smallness of my giving; I had been looking for a good excuse not to give much of my small income. But the speaker went on to say that the reason it is wicked to tithe is that this practice gives us the idea that we can pay God off with a straight ten-percent tip. As the speaker proceeded, I realized that I needed at least to get into the "wicked" category. As my wife and I began to give a larger portion of our income for religious purposes, I thought to myself: "This matter of religion really is important. I had better get deeper into the real business of it." And I started giving a great deal more time to reading the Bible, meditating on books of devotion, and praying. I found, as others have, that giving is a sacramental action which constantly reminds us of our commitment to God and of our need to relate to the Holy Creator. When we give to God and God's work, we are more likely to find ourselves in a closer relationship with the God who gives. God wishes to give us the full riches of divine grace.

Many of us have the muddle-headed idea that our possessions can save our souls. Only God can do that. We need to stop and reflect on how much we have and how much we really need. We also need to consider carefully how much we need to give and what people or projects need our help. Cornelius knew how to give wisely, and we need to attain the same wisdom.

Preparing for the Spiritual Journey

If we are to go far on the spiritual pilgrimage and find the love, peace, and power that are given by the Triune God, we need to make this venture a top priority in our lives and bring our entire being to the endeavor. I have been sketching out some guidelines for entering the narrow gate and following the difficult path that leads to eternal spiritual life. Let us pause a moment and meditate on the guidelines I have suggested. Which ones are we already following quite adequately? Are there some of these suggestions that we have never really considered? Which guideline is our top priority? It is revealing to rank these techniques in order of importance, for we all are at different places on the spiritual journey and so the way we rank them will differ for each of us. We need to honor people whose priorities are different from ours. Real fellowship requires understanding, and we do need a spiritual fellowship in which we share our priorities.

Let's list these practices so that we don't have to thumb back through the pages. When I started writing these guidelines, I found that I had not considered some of the most important practices for quite some time. It would be worthwhile to read over these suggestions several times quietly and see which ones touch us most deeply and need our greatest attention:

Act as though you believe in a spiritual realm.
Undertake the quest with serious purpose.

Seek out Christian fellowship and guidance for
    the journey.
Learn the mystery of silence.
Practice the art of Christian contemplation.
Learn the value of genuine Christian fasting.
Keep a record of your spiritual journey.
Be honest with yourself.
Love all other human beings as Christ has
    loved you.
Gird yourself with persistence and courage.
Give generously of your material goods and
    abilities.

You may wish to add other guidelines that you have found helpful, and you may also wish to delete one or two. These suggestions are the result of one person's attempt to enter the narrow gate and to help others do the same.

The pathway that Jesus sketched is not an easy one. You may quite legitimately ask why we should subject ourselves to such a strenuous undertaking. Would it not be better for me to tend my own garden and seize as much pleasure as I can and then die into oblivion? In some ways it might seem safer to avoid the spiritual journey and occupy ourselves with the physical world; this, in fact, is the tack taken by much of the Western world. Before we decide to follow the spiritual pathway, we need first ask if there is any valid alternative.

Most people in the West take it for granted that matter and the material world are essentially harmless. The idea is deeply rooted in Western culture that if we follow our concern about material things wherever it leads, all we will find in the end will be material blessings, an endless prospect of things like high-powered cars and wonder drugs.

And yet in just thirty years (1914-44) our rational and materialistic attitude dragged us through wars that created as much havoc as most of the other devastations in human history put together. How easily we forget. Any half-hearted attempt by Christian countries to follow the guidelines we have suggested would have eliminated the bloody, materialistic power catastrophe that convulsed our planet during this century.

Yet we try to forget these barbarities and go on treating matter as if we need look no farther in dealing with our responsibilities. By ignoring spiritual reality, we put ourselves in the position of the "boy Fausts" depicted by Gerald Sykes,[1] the scientists who are merely engaged in investigating matter and believe they carry no responsibility for the end product. If their discoveries are turned into bombs and dropped on innocent human beings, the blame belongs to someone else; their only concern is with the mysterious matter that appears to be inert and lifeless.

If there is no loving God, then there are no values, no standards, no ultimate love. Life ends at the grave. From this point of view, since physical life is extinguished at death people have no ultimate value or importance and can be destroyed by any power which wishes to do so. But God and the kingdom of heaven are there waiting to receive us.

The journey into the kingdom of heaven has very practical value. We have already pointed out the difficulties and dangers of pursuing the spiritual journey, but its value is equally clear and concrete.

If this spiritual journey is our destiny as human beings, we had better get on with it. The spiritual pathway into the kingdom of heaven described by Jesus[2] holds our only chance for full satisfaction as human beings, and it is unquestionably our best chance to continue as a viable and vital species. Only God, the ultimate center of creativity and love, can save us and through us save our world. In the process of seeking we are likely to find our original hope verified. Those who seek — who are willing to experiment and test their "hunch" — will likely come to know the God revealed in Jesus, just as we have been promised.

Notes

Introduction

1. Reynolds Price, *Three Gospels* (New York: Scribner, 1996). The essence of his profound Christian belief is stated on pp. 239-40.

2. David Gergen, "A Pilgrimage for Spirituality," *U. S. News and World Report*, December 23, 1996, p. 80.

3. See Chapter 6 in my book *Companions on the Inner Way: The Art of Spiritual Guidance* (New York: Crossroad, 1996).

4. David Gergen, "A Pilgrimage for Spirituality."

Act As if the Kingdom of Heaven Is Real

1. In my book *Can Christians Be Educated?* (Birmingham, AL: Religious Education Press, 1977), I sketched out a method for teaching the Christian faith. Chapters deal with education in prayer, in community, in service, in love, in finding meaning and value, and finding a world view with a place for the fullness of Christian life. In my book *Reaching: The Journey to Fulfillment* (Minneapolis, MN: Augsburg Fortress, 1994), I have developed these themes at greater length and in greater depth.

Undertake the Spiritual Quest with Serious Purpose

1. My wife describes this way of prayer on pp. 79-84 of my book *Reaching: The Journey to Fulfillment* (Minneapolis, MN: Augsburg, 1994).

2. The Greek word which is used to describe the spiritual path that we take after we enter the gate is *thlabo*. It means to be crushed, broken, oppressed. It describes well the persecution that the early Church endured; this may have been what Jesus was warning his disciples that they might face.

Seek Out Christian Spiritual Fellowship and Guidance

1. Adapted from Baron von Hügel, *The Mystical Element in Religion* (London: Dent, 1908), vol. I, p. 26.

2. *Daily Reflections of Carlo Carretto*, ed. by Father Joseph Diele (Hyde Park, NY: New City Press, 1996).

3. It is difficult to condense a two-hundred-page book into several paragraphs. I deal with the subject of fellowship on the spiritual journey in my book *Companions on the Inner Way* (New York: Crossroad, 1996). In that book, a long chapter provides a deeper insight into each of these five points of the star. I refer anyone interested in further understanding of any of these five points to this book.

Learn the Mystery of Silence

1. Thomas Carlyle, *Sartor Resartus*, Book III, Chapter III.

2. Soren Kierkegaard, *The Sickness unto Death* (published with *Fear and Trembling*) (Garden City, New York: Doubleday & Company, Inc., 1954), p. 198.

3. St. John of the Cross, *Dark Night of the Soul*, trans. E. Allison Peers (Garden City, NY: Doubleday & Co., Inc., 1959), pp. 67f.

Practice the Art of Christian Contemplation

1. An excellent short statement of the *lectio divina* and other forms of prayer is to be found in John Westerhoff, *Spiritual Life: The Foundation for Preaching and Teaching* (Louisville, KY: Westminster John Knox, 1994).

2. I have described my own method of pursing the spiritual journey in my book, *The Other Side of Silence* (Mahwah, NJ: Paulist Press, 1997). This book has recently been totally revised and re-edited.

Keep a Record of Our Spiritual Journey

1. I have written two books on the Christian interpretation of dreams: *Dreams: A Way to Listen to God*, (New York: Paulist Press, 1978); *God, Dreams and Revelation*, (Minneapolis, MN: Augsburg, 1991). In addition I have written a book on how to keep a religious record of our spiritual journey: *Adventure Inward: Christian Growth through Personal Journal Writing*, (Minneapolis, MN: Augsburg, 1980).

Love Others As Christ Has Loved Us

1. Rudolph Steiner, *Knowledge of the Higher Worlds and Its Attainment* (New York: AnthropoSophic Press, 1947), p. 40.

2. I have written three books that expand on the ideas presented here: *Can Christians Be Educated* (Birmingham, AL: Religious Press, 1977); *Caring, How Can We Love One Another* (New York: Paulist Press, 1980); *Set Your Hearts on the Greatest Gift* (Hyde Park, NY: New City Press, 1996).

3. Three books give an understanding of the vision and thought of Chiara Lubich. All of them can be obtained through New City Press, 202 Cardinal Road, Hyde Park, New York 12538. In *May They All Be One*, Chiara Lubich tells the story of how her vision began and grew. In *United in His Name*, Judith M. Povilus describes the experience and thought of Chiara Lubich. In *Chiara Lubich: A Life for Unity*, Chiara Lubich is presented in an interview with Franca Zambonini.

Gird Yourself with Persistence and Courage

1. In *Prayer and the Redwood Seed* (New York: Continuum Books, 1991) I have compared the growth of the soul to the growth of the ancient and gigantic redwoods from their tiny seeds.

Preparing for the Spiritual Journey

1. Gerald Sykes, *The Hidden Remnant* (New York: Harper and Brothers, 1962).

2. I have described the message in a book, *What Is Heaven Like?* (Hyde Park, NY: New City Press, 1997).